Ski Touring
Arizona

PLATEAUS OF SNOW

Ski Touring Arizona

BY DUGALD BREMNER

Northland Press Flagstaff, Arizona

Putting any book together is a group effort. Special thanks go to John Running and Sue Bennett for their wealth of technical advice, endless support, and aesthetic acuity.

Other thanks go to the many folks throughout the state who supported me with encouragement, logistics, information, equipment, and floors to sleep on.

Most of all, this book is dedicated to Jane.

Frontispiece: Tourer glides across meadows of Grand Canyon North Rim

Table of Contents

Enjoying ponderosa forest after a snowfall

Preface

I have qualms about writing this book. Who wouldn't? Anyone who has spent a lot of time and hard work to discover new and bewitching places out of doors has to feel some animosity toward guidebooks that open up those places to anyone.

This dichotomy exists for anyone who works in the outdoor industry, including wilderness guides, instructors, manufacturers and retailers of outdoor products, writers, and photographers. Why do we create an avenue for more people to come to the fragile places we love so much? The reason is because we do love these places.

It helps knowing that there are others who feel strongly about these powerful and needed places and who are concerned with seeing that these places stay as they are and as they are meant to be. As crowds and congestion continue to grow, it's important to know that we have somewhere to go and get away for an hour, for a month, for a year, or even forever. Like the support of a close friend, it is comforting to know it's there when you need it.

It is my hope that through the use of this guidebook, more people can strengthen their appreciation for the wilderness and become a part of those who choose to look to the future. After all, wilderness "belongs to all of us, and to none of us."

Dugald Bremner
Flagstaff, Arizona, 1987

Wing Mountain and San Francisco Peaks

Introduction

Snow may be one of Arizona's best-kept secrets. Not that it's really a secret, but the image of Arizona as the desert state is strong in the minds of many people. That most of Arizona's plateau country above 7,000 feet lies under a blanket of snow for a majority of the winter is news to most tourists and a surprising number of Arizonans. For some, the coming of snow and colder temperatures in the high country marks the end of outdoor recreation for the year, but for me, as well as many others, it only marks the beginning.

Cross-country skiing is perhaps the fastest growing winter sport these days. It's safe, inexpensive, accessible, easy to learn, and most importantly, lots of fun. Cross-country skiing is enjoyed wherever there is snow by people of all ages and abilities. For some, skiing allows off-season activity between dry season sports such as golf, tennis, jogging, or bicycling. Runners turn to groomed ski tracks in the winter for racing, while hikers ski to seek the stillness of winter solitude on a scenic summit. Some ski for therapy, some for social reasons, some for work, some as a means of getting in and out from a snow-bound cabin. To others, cross-country skiing is an end in itself. For the majority, however, cross-country skiing means simply taking an afternoon stroll to enjoy the winter woods and the fresh mountain air.

Whatever our reasons for taking to the snow in winter, this book was written to help ski enthusiasts of all ability levels enjoy Arizona's winter high country more efficiently and safely. The goal of this book is to encourage skiers to explore new places and to help increase awareness of and appreciation for the rich plateau country of Arizona.

This guidebook begins with pertinent information on ski touring in Arizona. In Part I, chapters on Arizona's snow climate and winter hazards contain important information for planning your ski tours. Other information on waxing, equipment, and preparing for tours will be of special interest to beginners. In Part II, ski tours are divided into regions. Information on how to use the tour descriptions is given at the beginning of this section. In the back of the book, a quick reference index can help readers find tours by region, difficulty, distance, or terrain.

With the information provided in this guidebook and a sense of adventure, you should be able to enhance your ski-touring experience in Arizona. As with most endeavors, there is no substitute for common sense and good preparation. So, ski safely and enjoy yourself.

Touring along creek at the base of Mormon Mountain

PART I

Preliminaries

SKIING IN ARIZONA

History

The snow fell hard in Flagstaff the winter of 1914–15. Deep drifts piled high in the streets, and the whole town closed its doors to winter except for two Norwegian immigrant brothers, Pete and Ole Solberg. With the heavy snows, things were slow in the carpentry business, yet Pete and Ole were busy with projects of their own. Using oak from the forest nearby, they fashioned four long, thin boards. Over a large pot of boiling water, they steamed the wood for several hours bending the ends into gentle curves. Using strips of leather tacked to the boards' midsections, they strapped the crafted wood to their boots and headed toward Mars Hill. This was the birth of skiing in Arizona.

With others eager to try this new sport, the Solberg brothers soon found they couldn't build enough skis for the demand. Eventually they persuaded a local merchant to order commercially made skis from Seattle at a cost of twelve dollars a pair.

Although skis made getting around in the winter much easier, few people used them for anything other than recreation. One exception was Gordon Evans, owner of the Mormon Lake Lodge from 1926 until 1944, who used skis out of necessity for working around the lodge in winter.

Caught one year by an early storm, Gordon and his helping hand Charley Simpson took off toward Flagstaff for supplies one morning by ski, hoping to stay at a neighbor's cabin halfway to town. Following Charley's advice, the skiers took a shortcut through the forest and in the thick of the storm became lost. Night fell and after frustrating efforts trying to light fires in the storm the two pressed on, coming across the cabin late that night. The following morning, Gordon continued to Flagstaff. Perhaps it was during this same storm that the Solberg brothers were called on to ski supplies to stranded sheepherders, snowed-in at their camp south of Flagstaff.

Norwegian-born
Ole Solberg at 94

Skiing was skiing in those days. Distinctions between downhill, touring, racing, or jumping skis were not yet made. As skiers took to the mountains, skiing up and sliding down, interest in building ski tows grew. With the use of lifts, skiers soon locked their heels down for stability and free-heel skiing fell to the wayside in Arizona. It wasn't until the 1960s that "modern" cross-country skis were introduced to Arizona when university professor Roger Thweatt brought his wooden touring skis to Flagstaff from Gunnison, Colorado. By the seventies, interest in hiking and backpacking had blossomed, and along with it, interest in nordic skiing. In 1973, the first annual Arizona Citizen's Cup cross-country ski race was held. Today, forest service ski trails, nordic touring centers, organized racing, and other facets of the sport continue to develop with the growing interest in cross-country skiing.

Arizona's Mountain Climate

Summer's end. The earth rocks back on its axis and the sun watches us from a more oblique angle, low in the sky. Evening comes earlier each day bringing with it the crisp cool air of the fall nights. On the peaks and plateaus, aspen leaves rise to a crescendo of color, turning from green to golden yellow, before dying and falling silently to the forest floor. Clouds come from the west, enshrouding the mountains; as quietly as they came, they move on, leaving behind the light dusting of the season's first snow. Winter has arrived.

Understanding the weather can make or break a ski outing. More than once, ski tourers have been caught too far out with inadequate clothing or equipment. Knowing the what's, where's, and when's of storm patterns and precipitation will help you in planning what to wear, where to go, and when to press on or turn back. Besides nightly news or radio broadcasts, local outdoor shops and the Weather Service are invaluable sources for current and expected weather conditions. The Arizona Department of Public Safety has information on road closures and conditions. (See page 133 for a list of important contacts.)

The climate of Arizona is as varied as its topography. It's not unusual to watch the weather change from clear skies to snow, rain, or hail, and back to sun again in the course of a day.

Arizona temperatures also fluctuate greatly, both seasonally and daily. With little atmospheric humidity to act as an insulator, radiant heat from the sun easily moves in and out through the atmosphere, heating the ground by day and radiating back out in the evening, leaving nights that are clear and cold. During the winter, temperatures on the plateaus can reach into the 70s during the day while plummeting at night to below freezing. Subzero temperatures are commonly recorded just north of Flagstaff. Daily temperature fluctuations are especially noticeable in the spring when cool nighttime temperatures freeze the slushy spring snow to ice, while warm daytime temperatures require light clothing and protection from the sun.

Along with temperature fluctuations, Arizona's snowy season varies greatly. Snowfall has been recorded as early as September and as late as June. Although the "normal" Arizona winter season in the mountains is between November and April, it isn't unusual for the season to begin as late as January. By late December and January, however, winter has usually begun in earnest, with cold, snowy storms hitting at a fairly regular rate. After a usual lull in February, winter picks up again in March, often bringing more snow than any other month of the year. By late April the spring skiing season is well under way, with occasional storms dropping snow at the higher elevations and cold rain at lower elevations.

Annual snow depths in the mountains range anywhere from eighty to 100 inches. Figures above and below this range are not unusual. Flagstaff records, for example, show snow accumulations of as little as eleven inches in 1934 and over 210 inches in 1973.

Although slight fluctuations in snowfall may vary from one winter to the next, the overall trend seems to be an increase in annual snowfall, as witnessed from the 1930s to the present. One of the major peaks in this changeable trend was in 1967 when over seven feet of snow fell in Flagstaff within a week! Such large and cold storms usually bring rare snows to the lower desert elevations. We encountered one such storm during a ski trip across the North Rim of the Grand Canyon. Having broken knee-deep powder for six days, we hurriedly dropped into the canyon to escape the snow and bathe in the warm desert temperatures. To our surprise, however, we awoke in the morning to find snow piled on our sleeping bags—it had snowed six inches at Phantom Ranch during the night!

Most of our winter storms come into Arizona from the west. Prevailing high-altitude winds from the north (the jet stream) direct cold, polar air masses south and east toward the state. These, in turn, are fed by warm moist air from Baja California. As these air masses collide, the warm air rises, expands, and cools. Combined with orographic lifting, lift from terrain features such as high plateaus and mountains, the moisture undergoes a series of changes, finally precipitating out as snow.

Early in the winter season, the storm track moves through the Pacific Northwest and across the Great Basin, losing much of its intensity as it encounters mountain ranges and other large topographic features. Weather from this track is marked by high winds and prolonged stormy periods of low intensity.

By mid-winter, the storm track has moved out over the Pacific Coast and follows a southerly route, allowing storms to load up with moisture before heading inland toward Arizona. This storm pattern brings us our classic heavy winter snows and accounts for about eighty percent of our winter storms. When the track is well developed, several storms may line up over the Pacific and hit Arizona in a continuous barrage of winter weather. In a good winter, this pattern may develop solidly and last from December through February.

During this period, storms often begin with a thin canopy of clouds at higher altitudes. Next to be seen are the long, lens-shaped lenticular clouds, forming at the tops of the mountains. Shaped by high winds, lenticular clouds are excellent telltale signs of impending storms. As the high clouds descend, snow begins to fall, often accompanied by high winds and a drop in temperature.

These large fronts come as a series of storm pulses alternating between thick whiteouts and light snow flurries. Eventually the clouds lift and the storm breaks; nights become clear and extremely cold, and the snowline recedes upward as daytime temperatures rise.

In the springtime, a third storm track develops. With a great influx of tropical air from the southwest, warmer and wetter storms come to the Arizona highlands. Heavy, wet snow falls during these storms, leaving a hard-to-ski snowpack of "mush" or "cement."

Arizona Snow

Having snow that changes quickly from powder to slush is the price we pay for living in a temperate climate. The soft powder you skied on in the morning may be heavy, wet "crud" by afternoon. While changeable snow conditions may be something we have to live with in Arizona, a little planning can ensure good skiing on any day of the ski season.

Elevation affects snow temperature: generally, the higher you go, the colder the snow. When conditions are crusty below, go higher to find colder, more powdery snow. When the higher snow has become crusty, the conditions below have probably improved to a firm, wet spring snow. In the spring, when it seems like the last of the storms has dropped its load on the mountains, keep your skis handy. Armed with a pair of shorts and some sunscreen, you can enjoy skiing on the upper reaches of the San Francisco Peaks or White Mountains on a firm base covered with a thin, slushy layer.

Sun exposure also influences snow conditions. When conditions on the south sides of hills seem thin and rocky, find a northern exposure where cooler temperatures and shade from the sun help the snow last longer. Even in the worst snow years, it is possible to find good skiing. Getting to know the areas where the snow is slow to melt will be useful when you are longing to ski.

WINTER HAZARDS

A fresh layer of soft, white snow lies in the forest; the cool mountain air rushes into your lungs; the touch of the morning sun warms your face. Heading out for the day, you effortlessly glide along enjoying the comfort of the morning and the company of family and friends. Certainly, cross-country skiing contains these and countless other qualities. Yet, like many endeavors, doing a ski trip involves taking on some risk. Along with that risk comes the responsibility of being aware of what you are doing, where you are going, and how to get there and back safely. What to expect in the way of weather, terrain, snow conditions, your own ability, and that of others with you are important considerations for your tour.

The purpose of this chapter is not to distract you from the enjoyment of cross-country skiing, but to make you aware of and respect the potential of the winter environment. As always, prevention of a potentially hazardous situation requires far less effort than dealing with its aftermath. The greater understanding and respect we have for the dynamic forces of nature, the longer we may enjoy its beauty and mystique.

Although it is beyond the scope of this guidebook to provide complete information on winter travel, there are a few things worth looking into while planning your ski tour. Most of the subjects below have been researched and written about extensively. A classic source of information on wilderness first aid is the book *Medicine for Mountaineering* put out by the Mountaineers of Seattle, Washington. If you are at all serious about the time you spend outdoors, you owe it to yourself and those with whom you travel to become familiar with potentially dangerous winter conditions.

Weather-Related Conditions

Dealing with cold weather keeps a lot of people at home in the winter, leaving the mountains open for those of us who enjoy uncrowded recreation. Being outside in cold weather doesn't mean being cold yourself. With proper clothing and preparation, going outside in wintertime can be as comfortable as staying inside, and more fun, too. Unfortunately, we are not always as prepared as we would like to be for any given condition. Sudden shifts in the wind, a drop in temperature, or worsening snow conditions can change the atmosphere of a tour. Knowing what to expect and how to deal with those changes can do more than affect your comfort outside; it can save lives.

HYPOTHERMIA   One of the major hazards that can arise due to cold is hypothermia. As the name suggests, hypothermia means a lowering of the body's core temperature. It is a serious, even lethal, condition that doesn't require extremely cold temperatures. Its onset can be sudden and unexpected.

In its early stages, hypothermia symptoms include slow movements and speech, shivering, poor coordination, coldness, and lack of responsiveness. During deeper stages of hypothermia, the victim takes on a paling of the skin, pupil dialation, weak pulse, and other shocklike symptoms.

Maintaining body heat is of primary importance when it is cold out. Remember, it is much easier to retain heat than to generate it, so when you stop for a rest put on more clothing BEFORE you get cold to prevent heat loss. Eating and drinking regularly and staying out of the wind are also good preventive measures.

Treatment for hypothermia should begin as soon as anyone notices they are getting too cold. The results of further cooling can be irreversible. The simplest treatment requires stopping any further cooling, then reheating the victim by external or internal (if conscious) sources. External sources of heat include warm, dry clothing, fire, or another's body heat. Warm, but not hot, liquids can be given internally along with carbohydrates to restore heat to conscious victims. When possible, get the victim to medical help or send for assistance.

FROSTBITE   Another subtle, cold-related medical hazard is frostbite, the freezing of tissue due to cold. Like hypothermia, frostbite is not restricted to the high-altitude mountaineer but can easily afflict the unwary skier out for an hour's tour. The extremities are affected first as the body tries to protect its core by keeping blood flow confined to the inner organs. Frostnip is the early stage of cooling where exposed areas—face, nose, ears—or the extremities—fingers and toes—become numb or tingly. Further cooling leaves the skin with a white, doughy appearance—the onset of actual freezing. While generally not fatal, frostbite can lead to infection and eventually to a loss of tissue or limb if not treated properly or in time.

Treatment for frostbite includes a rapid rewarming of the tissue by external sources. Placing the victim's extremity against another's stomach, armpit, or groin area adds a good source of external heat. Warm, not hot, water is also an excellent heating source. Never rub the frozen area, as it only creates further damage, and once thawed, never let the area refreeze. Transport the victim immediately to medical help.

By paying attention to early warning signs, frostbite can easily be avoided. With the first indication of numbness or discoloration, stop the tour and warm up the affected area. Change socks or gloves as they get wet. It's well worth a half-hour's break to save the loss of a toe, finger, or limb.

WIND, SUN, AND SNOW   Winter wind can affect a skier in many ways. The intense cooling effects of wind on air temperature are well documented and self-evident. As wind charts indicate, the speed of the wind can radically reduce air temperature. Protection from the wind with proper clothing or shelter can help prevent the chilling complications of hypothermia or frostbite. Other considerations from windy weather are an increased loss of body fluids, leading to dehydration, and windburn of the face and eyes, which can lead to temporary blindness. Wind in stormy weather can mean reduced visibility and disorientation.

The Arizona sun can be as devastating in the winter as it is in the summer.

With the white, snowy surface as a reflector, the sun's intensity is greatly magnified. I remember coming home from a spring day's skiing once with swollen, blistered lips—a victim of the reflected sun. Snowblindness, the eye's reaction to intense ultraviolet radiation, is a painful condition that can last for days. Swollen eyelids and extreme sensitivity can set in several hours after the actual exposure. A good pair of sunglasses that filter ultraviolet rays are useful when worn on a regular basis.

As large storms settle into the mountains in the winter, they bring with them potential hazards for the unprepared ski tourer. The prominent landmarks and trail so obvious one minute can be completely obscured the next by a descending storm. Following a route can be difficult during whiteout conditions when wind-blown snow obliterates ski tracks within minutes and reduces visibility to next to nothing. During these times, it is wise to stay on familiar ground and to rely heavily on your map and compass. Groups should ski together and keep from separating. The only thing harder than finding your own way out during a thick storm, is to have someone else trying to find you.

DEHYDRATION   Dehydration is a condition not commonly associated with winter; consequently, it is overlooked as a potential danger. Arizona's dry climate and intense sun enhance the loss of body fluids, especially during periods of intense physical activity. Drinking water or weak electrolyte liquids regularly is good preventive medicine. A common misconception is that water should be rationed, when, really, it is best used when needed. Eating snow only adds to the problem, as the energy used in melting the snow is greater than that received. A good trick for replenishing a dwindling water supply is to add small amounts of snow to your water bottle, and letting it melt by keeping the bottle warm as you ski.

Although injuries in cross-country skiing are few, they are something to keep in mind. Heavy, wet snow can lead to ankle strains or sprains. Knees are vulnerable to rocks and stumps in shallow snow, as are thumbs, wrists, and shoulders. As mentioned before, prevention is the best treatment for any situation. There is no substitute for being well versed in the first-aid treatment of injuries and conditions related to cold, windy weather.

Obstacles

ICE   Living in a temperate climate has its disadvantages when it comes to freezing water. Small bodies of water, such as cattle tanks and cinder-cone lakes, tend to freeze up fairly well in winter. Larger lakes, on the other hand, are less reliable. When lakes and ponds lie under a few feet of snow, it's a good bet they are frozen enough to hold your body weight, but it pays to be cautious just the same. This holds true especially in the fall and spring. Water freezes first along a lake's edge and more slowly in the deeper areas—something to keep in mind before heading out across a large open area.

OBJECTS   The excitement of an early storm brings many skis out of the closet and into the hills. Without a good base, however, rocks, stumps, and fallen trees not only tear up your equipment but you as well. Kneepads should be standard equipment for backcountry skiing, especially ski mountaineering. Once after a fresh snow, a hidden log took my knee out during a tour when we were still several miles from the car; a kneepad and some extra caution would have saved me a lot of agony and time out from skiing.

Perhaps worse than the natural obstacles are the man-made ones, such as fences and sign posts. Even when the snow is deep, barbed wire fences lie like booby traps under the surface. Cinder pits should also be approached with caution, as rocks and debris can easily cause bodily injury. Always check an area for fences and other hidden objects before skiing.

Never ski downhill toward a fence; ski down slowly at an angle. The best way to cross a fence is to find a low spot, take off your skis, and climb over. If the fence is buried enough, it may be possible to step over sideways, using your poles and a fence post for balance.

Avalanches

If the idea of snow in Arizona seems unusual to some people, the fact that there are avalanches here must seem unbelievable. However, on the San Francisco Peaks alone there are over sixty-six recognized avalanche paths. Other paths exist on steep slopes in the White Mountains, such as on Mt. Baldy. Avalanches are a very real part of the Arizona high country, and while there have been no skier-related fatalities to date due to avalanche burial, the increasing numbers of skiers touring the high backcountry and skiing steep terrain make the potential ominous.

Avalanche statistics are grim: one of every ten skiers caught in an avalanche is killed; no one has ever survived a burial of over six feet; most avalanche victims triggered the slide that buried them; after thirty minutes, survival chances drop to below fifty percent.

This section on avalanches by no means covers all you need to know for avalanche safety. Much has been written on the subject, and it is strongly recommended that anyone who likes to leave the flats for steeper terrain should learn more about the behavior of the snow on which they are skiing. Perhaps the best information for the ski tourer on the subject of avalanche safety and behavior is in the pocket-sized book *The ABC of Avalanche Safety*, by E. R. LaChappelle.

Avalanches, like hurricane winds or flooding rivers, carry a devastating power within them. Simply put, avalanches occur when the weight of snow accumulation exceeds the mountain's ability to hold it in place. Snow, under gravity's influence, breaks loose and builds up speed and power, moving house-sized boulders, snapping mature trees in half, and obliterating everything in its path, until coming to rest on the flats below.

Avalanches come in a variety of forms, sizes, and shapes. They can release from a small point, building as they descend, or take off as a large slab, hundreds of feet across. They can comprise the top three inches of loose snow from the last storm, or "run to the ground," carrying along a whole season's worth of snowpack. Mid-winter avalanches tend to fall in a billow of dry snow, choking the air with a flourlike powder of snow crystals, while the wet snow avalanches of spring tend to rumble down in large truck-sized blocks of a broken slab.

Wind, water, temperature, snow structure, and snowpack all play a part in determining the avalanche potential at any given moment. Their interaction is an interesting science in itself, yet knowing some general rules of snow behavior can be useful.

When new snow falls, it forms a bond with the snow already on the surface. This bond may be strong or weak, depending on the structure of the snow crystals and the temperature at which they fell. A good bond means a more stable snowpack, hence lower avalanche danger, while a poor bond creates a weak or unstable layer in the snowpack, a potential for release.

Avalanches most commonly occur during or just after a heavy storm. Generally, any storm depositing over one inch an hour or twelve inches per storm is considered hazardous in avalanche country. This hazard is further compounded by wind that can build large cornices on the leeward sides of ridges and hang precariously over a potential avalanche chute. The steepness of a slope also contributes to avalanche danger. Slopes of thirty-five to sixty degrees build up and run most frequently; steeper slopes tend to drop constantly, preventing buildup, while shallower angles tend not to slide. Other factors, including snow density and moisture content, also affect the stability of the snowpack.

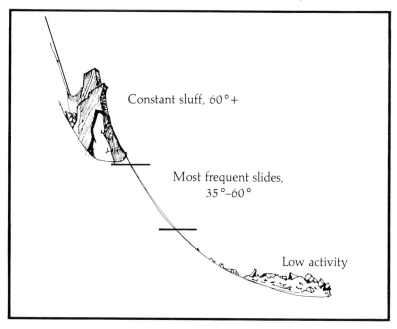

Constant sluff, 60°+

Most frequent slides,
35°–60°

Low activity

More important than understanding how avalanches work is knowing how to recognize and avoid them. On the San Francisco Peaks, most major avalanche chutes are easily recognizable as large swaths that start well above treeline and plummet down, cutting deep into the trees below. In the drier seasons, the effects of avalanches can be seen by exploring these chutes. Stands of trees mowed off to uniform height, young trees deformed and bent downhill, or boulders and other debris collected at the bottom of the chute mark the avalanche's devastating path.

The best way to survive an avalanche is, of course, not to go near one to begin with. Avalanches may be triggered directly by snowfall, a rise in temperature, loud noise, or the weight of a skier.

The starting zone of an avalanche path presents the most danger to the ski tourer. Descending in elevation and danger are the track and runout zones of an avalanche chute. The safest place to avoid these areas is to circle high above the starting zone, on a safe ridge, or well below the runout zone.

If crossing these zones is unavoidable, cross one at a time; better to have others free to help if the slope runs. Skiing in the trees can reduce—though not eliminate—your chances of starting a slide. Take the precaution of loosening pack straps and removing poles from your wrists, then move quickly across the suspect slope until you reach a safe spot in the trees on the other side.

If caught, relax and try to swim on the surface. When moving snow stops, it hardens quickly into a cementlike consistency, so keep one hand over your mouth for a breathing pocket and thrust the other up to help others find you.

If you see someone else caught, DON'T GO FOR HELP, but make a quick search when it is safe. Watch the path of the victim's movement intently: mark the point where they were caught by the slide and the point where they were last seen on the surface, then search below with a pole or probe. A trail of clothing and other debris can help lead toward the victim.

With a little planning and common sense, you can make your tour into the backcountry a safer one. First and foremost, never ski alone. Carry emergency equipment, especially a shovel. Consult with the weather service and local ski patrol for updates on conditions. Always leave a tour route and schedule with someone for rescue purposes. Best of all, be responsible for yourself and your group by being alert to signs of snow conditions. Look and listen for signs of settling snow. The "whump" sound of a settling snowpack can indicate a weak layer below—definitely a bad sign. Watch for fracturing snow under your skis as you ski along. Snow dropping from trees or snowballs growing as they roll downhill are also telltale signs of settling snow. In the high country, look at existing chutes for recent activity. Checking a slope by carefully breaking off a cornice can give you an idea, although inconclusive, on how stable conditions are. The best advice is, when in doubt, go around the questionable area or ski elsewhere.

When it comes down to it, you are your best resource for safety in the backcountry. Be responsible and don't take unnecessary chances. Ski safely and ski again another day.

PREPARING FOR YOUR TOUR

Skis

Since the introduction of synthetic touring skis in the early seventies, the cross-country ski industry has seen tremendous growth in interest and technology. The development of lighter and stronger touring equipment has allowed great diversification in the skier's potential and ability; nordic skiers are doing things and going places not thought possible before.

Between the extremes of mountaineering and ski-skating, there is a growing continuum of equipment for all styles and levels of cross-country skiing. At the lighter end of the spectrum are track skis. This includes racing and training skis for use on machine-groomed ski trails. Skis in this category are designed for speed and light weight. Track skiing can give a sensation of effortless skiing and is a good place to practice technique and ski without worry of where to go.

Early model skis (1920s)

Touring skis constitute the next category of cross-country skis. This broad area of skiing includes skis that can be used in and out of groomed trails as well as for light backcountry skiing. Stronger and lighter touring skis are constantly being developed in this largest area of the cross-country skiing market. The technology allows us to ski longer with less effort in more conditions than ever before. With a few exceptions, most of the tours in this book can be done on light touring skis.

At the heavier end of things are mountaineering skis. Skis here are built wide for stability and flotation and have metal edges to bite in icy or packed snow conditions. Although many skis with these characteristics are made with a softer flex and are lightweight for touring the backcountry, several manufacturers make skis for nordic downhill use in alpine ski areas. These skis are similar in flex and weight to alpine skis and are poorly suited to backcountry use.

A WORD ON WOOD   As with many sports, the use of synthetics in cross-country ski construction has put the production of wooden skis on the wane, ending an era of another handcrafted natural product. While synthetic skis improve handling characteristics and strength of a ski, they escape the essence and elegance of a well-crafted wooden ski. Though technology has changed, snow hasn't, and wooden skis still work well and are a joy to ski on. In the hope of not seeing the wooden ski die out completely, I encourage you—if you are a craftsperson, a diehard, or simply a romantic—to find a pair or two and keep them around. When the snow is cold and soft, go for a tour, carve some gentle turns, and remember what nordic skiing is all about.

Waxing

Fresh snow last night, the morning sky is clear and sunny. Grabbing your skis and friends, you take off for a day's tour through the woods. As the day warms, a rain of wet snow falls from the trees, and your skis grow heavy and slow as you pass from sun to shade. Suddenly, progress stops; looking down you see a cubic yard of snow stuck to the bottom of each ski. Sound familiar? Let's take a look a some ways of dealing with variable snow conditions.

Waxless skis have come a long way. Every year improvements are made that allow waxless skis to perform more like a properly waxed ski. Even today, however, waxless performance tends to drop off in extreme snow conditions. Where they do best is in the middle temperatures, around the transition from melt to freeze and vice versa. In Arizona, these temperatures are common; hence many skiers have gone waxless for general touring.

Slow, waxless ski bases can be made faster by applying teflon or silicon liquids. This also helps prevent icing, the condition descibed above, which occurs as wet snow under trees freezes onto your skis, then picks up the colder snow as you ski into the open areas.

The goal of waxing is to maximize both the grip and the glide of your skis. As a ski glides, it melts the snow underneath and rides on a thin layer of water.

Shift your weight to that ski to kick off, and you press the wax into the crystals of snow allowing the ski to grip the snow. When you wax a ski you are trying to match the wax to the snow crystal. Wet snow has rounded crystals and needs a soft wax. Fresh snow is dry with sharp crystals and needs a hard wax to match it.

Waxing can be simple. Ski waxes come in color-coded cans that correspond to various snow conditions and air temperatures. Waxes may vary from one brand to the next, but in general, greens and blues work for fresh, cold snow; violet for temperatures around freezing; reds and yellows for warmer, wet snow. In Arizona, most conditions can be covered by using blue for cold snow soon after a storm, violet as the snow starts to melt, and red for wet snow that hasn't refrozen or metamorphosed (see klisters below). Another option is to use one of several two-wax systems, one wax for wet snow and one for dry. These systems are simple and work fairly well.

Wax can be rubbed on the ski base like a crayon starting at the heel and moving forward. Make a few thin layers, smoothing them out in between with a cork or hand. Variations in the length and thickness of wax application affect how a particular wax will work.

Klister comes from the Swedish word meaning glue. With a consistency of honey, klisters come in color-coded tubes and are designed to be used when snow has melted and refrozen—a common occurence in this region—and under icy and wet, springlike conditions. Klister skiing is fast and enjoyable. Learning to use it allows you to enjoy much more of the ski season. Apply klister sparingly in short strokes or squiggles under the foot, generally from the heel forward, then smooth out. As with waxes, start with colder klisters and change to softer as needed. Generally, purple and red klisters work well for most snow conditions in Arizona; blue klister is used in icy conditions.

Here are some general rules to keep in mind for waxing:
- Apply wax in many thin layers rather than in one thick one;
- Not enough kick? Apply wax thicker, then try longer (forward), then change to a softer wax;
- Add soft wax over hard, not vice versa;
- Start out with colder waxes; it's easier to add wax than it is to scrape it off and start over.

The best way to learn waxing is to experiment. Start simple and add waxes to your kit as you need them. Talk to local specialty shops to get information particular to the area.

Clothing

In the words of outdoorsman and philosopher Larry Coats, "There is no such thing as bad weather, there's just bad clothing." If you think about it, he's right. We are adaptable creatures by virtue of our technology and creativity. For the ski tourer, this means looking outside and thinking about what the day might bring in the way of weather. My amendment to Larry's statement is, "Better to have it with you and not need it, than to need it and not have it." This applies especially to clothing, food, and emergency gear.

Dressing for any outdoor activity can be summed up in one word: layering. This means dressing by combining several garments rather than wearing one thick one. Consider the down jacket. When you ski, you warm up and get hot with the jacket on. Take it off, and you are too cold. It's all or nothing with no in-between. By wearing layers, you can mix and match clothing to the right climatic conditions.

Clothes can be considered in two categories, insulative and protective. The former, long underwear, sweaters,and such, add warmth by creating dead air space, which is warmed by your body. Wools are still great for insulative wear. Many new synthetics, such as polypropylene and pile, are light, quick drying, and warm even when wet. Cotton, on the other hand, can't be relied on in foul weather, because it loses warmth when wet, and in the winter, DRY means WARM.

Protective clothing is the wind and waterproof gear that protects your insulative clothing from the elements. In winter, wear a breathable garment for your protective layer that doesn't trap perspiration inside, yet protects you from the snow and wind.

For most conditions, I wear a light layer against my skin, with a medium and heavier layer above. A windshell and an extra sweater are handy when I stop to rest or if the temperature drops. Put extra clothing on AS SOON AS YOU STOP when it is cool; it's better to maintain the body heat you have worked for, than to cool down and have to regenerate it. Hats and gloves are a must, of course, and carry an extra pair of dry mittens and socks; fingers and toes go fast when it's cold.

Because clothing materials and designs change every year, ask your local outdoor shop for the best options in ski clothing. Although some garments are made for specific conditions, many can be used for a lot of activities —mountain biking, backpacking, hiking—throughout the year.

Et cetera

What to carry on your tour depends on several factors such as tour length, how far from the car you will be, the ski terrain, and your group's ability. Water and food provide necessary refueling. Sun protection, such as hats, cream, and glasses, is a must when out on the reflective snow. A map and compass are important for safety as well as useful for getting to know the surrounding country. For backup situations, spare ski parts, repair, and first aid kits can keep a fun tour from turning into an epic.

Like clothing, ski equipment changes seasonally. Take adequate gear for the terrain you plan to tour. Don't get stuck on an icy downhill with racing skis or lug mountaineering equipment around on flats unnecessarily.

ETHICS AND TOURING

Cross-country skiing's steady rise in popularity sends more and more people gliding through the trails and backcountry of Arizona's forests. Coming across other groups of skiers and sharing the enjoyment of the winter woods has become a part of the touring experience at many popular areas. However, along with sharing the forests with other tourers, there comes a responsibility to maintain the quality of the outdoors so that it is there for us to enjoy later. While there are no rules in the ski touring world as there are in alpine skiing, common sense and consideration can go a long way in helping to maintain a quiet intrusion on the outdoors and on anyone there enjoying it.

Aside from ATC's and snowmobiles, dogs are propably the most touchy topic among ski tourers. Dogs are fun to have along on a tour, but unfortunately, paws punch holes in the tracks and tear up the skiing surface, reducing ski grip and glide while increasing skier frustration. I have a dog who loves to go along on tours in the winter, and I often take her with me. But when skiing at popular areas, especially on marked trails or at touring centers, I leave her behind. Other times she joins me on tours to more remote spots in the forest.

Leaving your dog behind may seem hard to do, but even harder is having to ask someone to please not let their dog on the ski trails. Confrontations often lead to bad feelings or even worse. So help out by leaving pets at home unless you are going to a place where no one else will be skiing.

What would you do if a jogger off the street ran up to your house and made himself comfortable on your front porch? Or maybe if he came inside and helped himself to a glass of water and warmed himself up by your fire? Seems unlikely, but this is something private land owners living in the forests have to deal with each winter. Something about a cabin in the woods seems inviting to most people for a lunch stop or refuge from the cold, but being in or on someone's cabin is tresspassing whether you are disrupting anything or not. Private cabins are scattered throughout the forests, some as summer homes and others as permanent dwellings. Whatever their state of use, they are not public domain and should be left alone and have their privacy respected.

Skier responsibility also takes place off the skis and on the roads, especially where parking and driving are concerned. Parking on winter roads in this state is scarce. Since skiers come and go at different schedules, it is important not to block others in while you are on a tour. If space is limited, take the responsibility to dig your own spot. The department of transportation requires that vehicles be parked at least ten feet off the pavement.

Another vehicle problem involves their use on snow-covered dirt roads. Torn up tracks and muddy ruts make skiing difficult and only save the driver a few minutes of ski time. Unfortunately, most of the offenders here aren't skiers, but it is something to be aware of all the same. Unless roads are uncovered, park and ski in. After all, it's what we came here for anyway.

NIGHT SKIING

The squeak of cold leather and the sound of wood sliding on snow break the stillness of the night. The moon, now full and high above the skyline, drapes its blue hue like cloth across the smooth snow. From beneath the snow's glittering surface, ski tips emerge and sink with each step, leaving shadowy traces behind. These are memories of my first cross-country tour at night. Every season I make a point of touring under the full moonlight, partly for its refreshment and invigorating qualities and partly to remind me of my introduction to the winter backcountry.

Night skiing adds a new dimension to nordic skiing. With consideration of where and when to go, it is something to be experienced for tourers of all ability levels. In general, clear moon-filled nights are best for ski touring. A bright moon reflected off the snow enhances visibility and creates an exhilarating atmosphere for a tour. Despite the brightness, depths and distances can be misleading at night, so look for open parks or prairies free of rocks, fences, and other obstacles. If skiing far from your vehicle, ski in a group to prevent getting lost, especially if there are less experienced skiers along.

Clear nights usually bring cold air, so plan ahead by packing extra clothing and snacks for rest stops. Warm drinks like cocoa, tea, or spiced wine add an important part to any moonlight tour. Other useful items to carry are flashlights, maps, and matches.

For starters, there are several good touring spots in the Flagstaff area off U.S. 180 with excellent moonlight touring terrain, such as Wing Mountain (tour, page 38) or the open parks near Kendrick Peak (tour, page 45). Government Prairie also offers great potential for nighttime skiing (page 85).

Most of the tours near Greer are plenty open for good night skiing, especially on the open parks near Pole Knoll (page 95) and Greens Peak (page 98). Near Alpine, try skiing in Williams Valley (page 106) or go up to the fields by Hannagan Meadow (tour, page 111) for a good moonlight tour.

Touring to Walker Lake, North Hart Prairie Road

Arizona

Grand Canyon

REGION 1

Flagstaff ●

Heber ●

REGION 3

REGION 2

Greer ●

Phoenix ●

Tucson ● REGION 4

PART II:

The Tours

HOW TO USE THIS GUIDEBOOK

The tour areas of this guidebook are divided into four sections: northern Arizona, the White Mountains, Mogollon Rim, and southern Arizona. With the San Francisco Peaks at its hub, the northern Arizona region extends west to Williams, east to Highway 89 North, north to the Grand Canyon, and south to Mormon Lake. The White Mountain region follows the highlands to the Mogollon Rim country south of Alpine and west past Greer toward Heber. The Mogollon Rim region covers the Forest Lakes area west of Heber and extends toward Baker Butte above Payson on the rim. The section on southern Arizona includes the unique highlands of the Santa Catalinas, the Chiricahua Mountains, and Mt. Graham. These areas were chosen because of their scenic value and reliability for snow. Although there are several other good areas for touring in Arizona, most of them lie at lower elevations, which require a good snow year for skiing, one example being the higher reaches of the Bradshaw Mountains south of Prescott. Other areas were left out of this guidebook because of heavy use by snowmobile and other off-road vehicles. The combination of tight, icy roads and blind corners can make skiing in snowmobile areas hazardous. With growing interest in nordic skiing, it is hoped that there will be a growing demand for separate vehicle and skier-use areas.

Each tour is classified according to the terrain difficulty, the distance covered, and the time it takes to complete the tour. These variables are further described in the following section. Route descriptions for tours begin at parking areas and either lead to specific destinations or describe round-trip routes. Tours are accompanied by information on human and natural history and other special interests along the route.

Terrain

Using the symbols common to all ski areas, nordic or alpine, skiers can assess the difficulty of the terrain for each tour. This rating does not account for any

21

side jaunts that may be taken from a given tour. Also, the terrain descriptions do not take into account the distance covered on a particular tour. In other words, a tour with an "Easier" terrain rating may cover many miles and take most of the day to do and would not be recommended for novice skiers. Similarly, a short tour that only covers a few miles might have a rating of "More Difficult," which would require some intermediate skiing experience. In general, however, the terrain ratings are defined as follows.

 EASIER: Flat or rolling terrain. Hills with easy climbs and gentle runouts.

 MORE DIFFICULT: Terrain with steeper climbs and descents as well as possible maneuvering among obstacles such as rocks, trees, or windy roads.

 MOST DIFFICULT: Extremely steep climbs and descents encountered. Practical knowledge of backcountry skiing techniques required. Tight maneuvering in trees or rocks probable.

Forest Service trail marker for cross-country skiing

Time

The pace at which we choose to tour is a matter of personal preference; hence, the time it takes to do a tour can vary greatly depending on snow conditions, weather, the number of rest or lunch stops, a skier's experience, physical shape, and general attitude. I have tried to give average times, based on a moderate pace and ability level. When in doubt, always allow more time than anticipated.

The table below illustrates the expressions of time used in this guide. Times are expressed relative to the amount of day the tour requires rather than in actual hours, to allow for the above-mentioned variables. In general, a short tour will take one to three hours, a full-day tour will take six to ten hours.

Type of Tour	Approx. no. of hours
Short	1–3
Half-day	3–5
Full day	6–10
Multiday	10+ (requires overnight provisions)

Distance

Distances are given in round-trip miles, unless otherwise indicated. Distances are often broken down into segments within the tour description itself. Although these distances have been measured, they should only be treated as close approximations. Besides that, distances seem to have a way of lengthening on the uphills and in the afternoons.

Maps

The maps in the book indicate the general layout of the area, showing major features and tour direction. They should not be relied upon for navigation, especially for longer, more complicated tours.

Maps are essential for safe ski touring. They don't weigh much, are easy to carry, and are a fun and useful way to get to know the country around you. Forest service maps are inexpensive and show most of the roads and geographic features in a very large area, yet do not indicate terrain very well. Geological survey topographic maps, on the other hand, are the best for showing topography. Gas station maps are good for getting you from one region to the next but they are best left in the glove box of your vehicle while you ski. In this guide, both topographic map (USGS) and forest service map (USFS) names are given for each tour.

Northern Arizona

SAN FRANCISCO PEAKS

Heading west on my way to college, I caught my first view of the San Francisco Peaks, silhouetted against a classic Arizona sunset. The hitchhiker I had picked up earlier told me the peaks were so named because on a clear night you could see the lights of San Francisco from their summit. I spent the better part of the next day huffing and puffing my way up the mountains and then waited for night to fall. Aside from some cabins scattered in the forest below, the only lights I saw were those of the crisp celestial canopy above. However, with the morning's rising sun, I discovered the broad expanse of high plateau country that surrounds the San Francisco Peaks, a more brilliant and rewarding view than the lights of any city.

The San Francisco Peaks near Flagstaff are many things to many people. To the Navajo and Hopi, they are the Sacred Mountains, home of the kachinas. To the early explorers and settlers of the region, they were a prominent landmark, to others, a highland oasis from the heat of the surrounding deserts. To ski tourers, the peaks offer several thousand square miles of touring possibilities from casual tours on the snow-covered roads of its rolling foothills, to steep ski mountaineering on its summit slopes.

Nuva-teekia-ovi, or "Place of Snow on the Very Top," is the name the Hopi tribe gave the mountain centuries ago. To the Navajo, they are *Do'ko' oslid,* or "Abalone Shell Mountain" or "Blue Western Mountain." The Havasupai call them the "Big Rock Mountains" or "Mountains of Virgin Snow," *Huehhassahpatch.* These are the oldest names for the peaks. When the Spanish began filtering into the Southwest during the sixteenth century, the name *Sierra Sin Agua,* or "Mountain Without Water," was aptly applied to the porous massif. The present name for the peaks came from the Hopi village of Oraibi in 1629 when visiting Franciscan missionaries named them in honor of their patron saint and, possibly, to help establish Christian dominance over the local tribes by replacing the Indian name with one of Christian origin.

Like a grand staircase from the sky, the four summits that make up the San Francisco Peaks descend in a sweeping arc from the north. Humphreys, the highest point in the state (12,633 feet), was named in 1872 for the topographic engineer and captain of the Ives Expedition, Brigadier General Andrew A. Humphreys. Humphreys, who assessed data from survey trips through the area, probably never saw the peak that carries his name. Agassiz Peak (12,356 feet) was named in honor of Jean Louis Randolphe Agassiz, the Harvard professor and

24

Cinder cones of the San Francisco Volcanic Field after a snowstorm

Swiss zoologist who passed through the area in 1867 doing fossil studies for a railroad survey. John C. Fremont was the namesake for the third highest of the peaks, Fremont Peak (11,969 feet). Sarcastically nicknamed the Pathfinder of the West (he was always lost), Fremont was well known for his explorations of routes through the West, yet like Humphreys, it is doubtful he ever set foot in this part of the country. At 11,460 feet, Doyle Peak is the lowest of the San Francisco Peaks, yet it is the only one of the four summits that is actually named for a local pioneer. Besides making his living as a cattleman, Allen Doyle guided in the area for such people as the famed western novelist Zane Grey.

From a distance, the broad slopes of the San Francisco Peaks rise evenly until they are broken by the jagged line that joins the four mountain summits. It is as though the symmetry of the mountain was interrupted by some cataclysmic event, which, in fact, it was. The San Francisco Peaks are what remains of a large stratovolcano, one whose formation comes from flows of lava alternating with explosions of volcanic fragments. Its summits form the uncollapsed rim of the volcano that had its heyday within the last two million years. Projecting the present lines of its slopes upward would place the original summit 2,500 feet higher than its present height.

The San Francisco Peaks and its surrounding lava flows and cinder cones constitute the San Francisco Volcanic Field. With the peaks at the center of activity, over 400 other vents poured forth thick beds of lava and built rounded cinder cones that covered the area with volcanic material for tens of miles in all directions.

In contrast to their fiery origin, the San Francisco Peaks underwent glacial activity during the late Pleistocene. Glaciers of 100 yards deep and five miles long moved down from their cirques. Sculpted landforms and morrains can be seen today on tours to the higher reaches of the mountain.

SAN FRANCISCO PEAKS WEST

U.S. Highway 180

Highway 180 from Flagstaff to the Grand Canyon winds across the rolling plateau of the west slope of the San Francisco Peaks. Along the way, snow-covered roads disappear into the woods, and glimpses of the peaks dominate the skyline. This is Flagstaff's backyard for ski touring; ranging from a thousand to two thousand feet above town, the area along U.S. 180 offers the most reliable and accessible snow in the Flagstaff region. Even in low snow years, when the weather is springlike in town, it is possible to find snow in this area. In general, the farther north you go, the better the snow.

Presently, there is little plowed parking along the highway, however, it is usually possible to get off the road far enough to park. Carry a good shovel with you for such occasions. If parking on the highway shoulder, you need to be four feet from the pavement. Plowed parking is available at Shultz Pass Road, Hidden Hollow Road, Snow Bowl Road, Hart Prairie Road, Wing Mt. Road, just past FS 193 near Deer Tanks, and beyond North FS 151.

The tours in this section range from short to full day, and easier to more difficult terrain. Tours are organized from Flagstaff northward.

Bristlecone pine, the oldest known living organism, on the upper reaches of the San Francisco Peaks

Schultz Pass

TERRAIN: **More Difficult**   TIME: **Half-day**
DISTANCE: **3.5 miles** one way
MAPS: **USGS—Flagstaff West, Humphreys Peak, Sunset Crater West,
        Flagstaff East**
   USFS—Coconino

Schultz Pass forms the broad saddle joining Mt. Elden to the San Francisco Peaks. Schultz Pass gets its name from a sheepman who used the springs at the top of the pass for his sheep.

To get to Schultz Pass, turn off of U.S. 180 onto forest service road (FS) 420, .1 mile past the Museum of Northern Arizona, and follow it for one mile until it reaches a gate marking its winter closure. From here, a slow climb for 3.5 miles leads to the open highlands of Schultz Pass. Like other tours close to town, Schultz Pass is best for touring during a good snow year or soon after a storm. Besides a popular touring spot, Schultz Pass Road is often used by snowmobile and ATC traffic. Caution should be used when returning down their icy tracks.

Besides a destination in itself, Schultz Pass is a good jumping-off point for other tours. Just before reaching the pass itself, FS 789 heads to the right as Schultz Pass Road makes a prominent left-hand bend. This road climbs for a mile to the serene meadows of the Dry Lake Hills, a popular browsing spot for deer and elk. Other tours toward the San Francisco Peaks, Inner Basin, or Freidlein Prairie are possible.

Farther along Schultz Pass Road, just past the man-made Schultz Tank, a road branches northward to join the old Weatherford Road. High above, this road can be seen switchbacking up Weatherford Canyon toward Fremont Peak. The Weatherford Road was built in 1926 as a toll road to the top of the peaks. John W. Weatherford, proprietor of the toll road, the Weatherford Hotel, and Flagstaff's Opera House (presently the Orpheum Theater), built the road as a commercial enterprise after hiking to the top himself and being struck with the view. The venture faded with time, and the area is presently the summer site of the annual War Dog foot race, a fifteen-mile round-trip race from Schultz Pass up to the Humphrey-Agassiz saddle and back.

The east side of Weatherford Canyon is formed by Schultz Peak, a volcanic blister on the side of the San Francisco Peaks. Schultz Peak was the temporary site of Lowell Observatory in 1922.

Schultz Pass

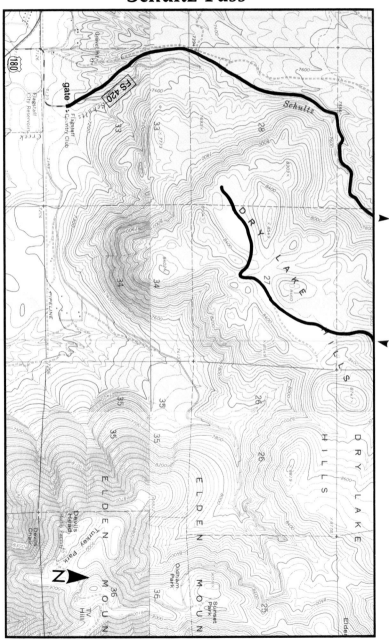

MAP 1 OF 2

Schultz Pass

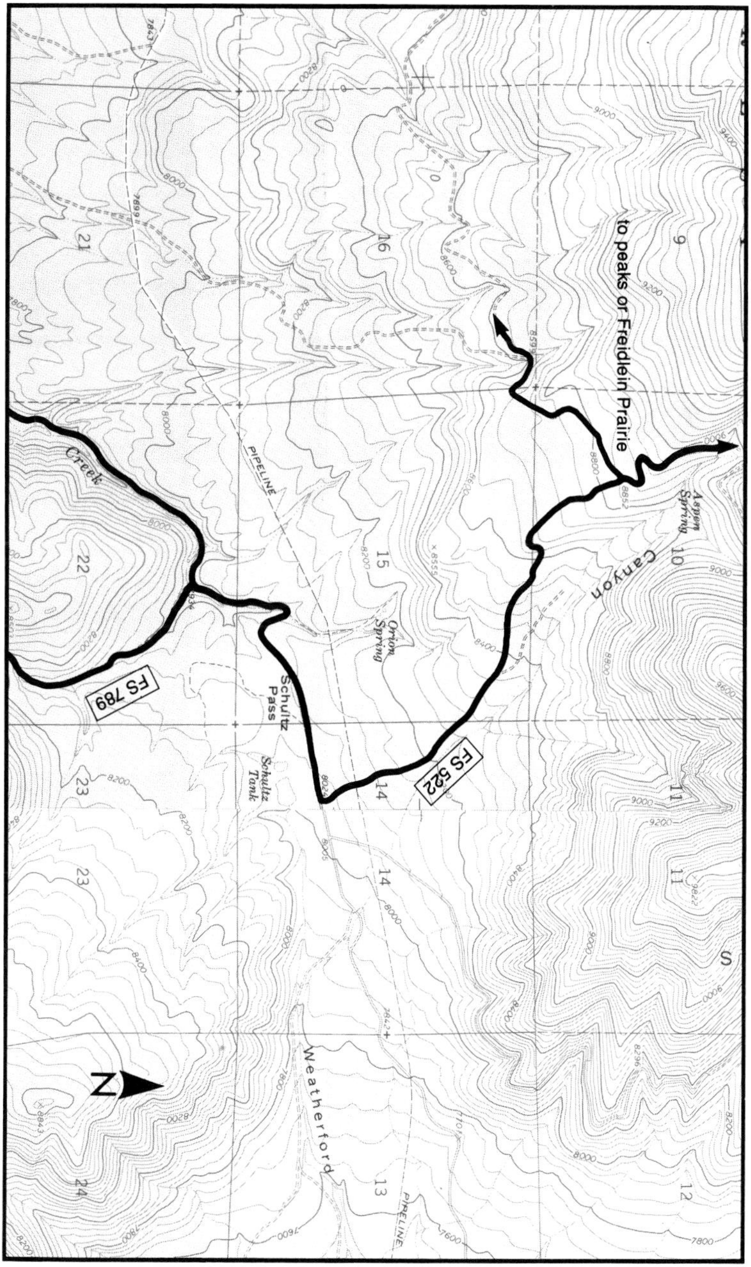

MAP 2 OF 2

Hidden Hollow

TERRAIN: **Easier**   TIME: **Short Day**
DISTANCE: **2 to 3 miles**
MAPS: **USGS—Flagstaff West**
　　　USFS—Coconino

As the name implies, Hidden Hollow is tucked away at the side of U.S. 180, 1.5 miles north of Flagstaff. This is a convenient spot for a morning's ski and holds snow suprisingly well for being so close to town. A sign marks the entrance to Hidden Hollow Road (FS 506), which leads to a small development in the forest. Much of the area is private land, and care should be taken not to tresspass or disrupt the residences there so that skiing in the adjacent forest will always be available.

A short distance up Hidden Hollow Road, a gas pipeline road, marked by orange and white iron gates, parallels the Hidden Hollow Road on the left. Park here and walk or ski past the gates (depending on snow conditions), then follow the pipeline up a short but steep hill. While the ski up the hill is steep, the terrain above is gentle and easy to ski. On top, sparsely forested land offers scenic touring south and west toward A-1 Mountain, a large cinder cone perched on the edge of Fort Valley. A number of dirt roads provide good touring through the forest. Return by a short walk or ski down pipeline hill.

Hidden Hollow

Freidlein Prairie

TERRAIN: **Easier to More Difficult** TIME: **Half-day**
DISTANCE: **5 miles**
MAPS: **USGS—Humphreys Peak**
      USFS—Coconino

Visible from the town of Flagstaff is a large triangular meadow along the lower southern slopes of the San Francisco Peaks. Freidlein Prairie, named for an early pioneer and rancher, is a broad, open-forested prairie with spectacular touring possibilities and easy access.

Snow Bowl Road lies seven miles north of Flagstaff off of U.S. 180. Two and a half miles up the Snow Bowl Road, FS 522 leaves to the east (right). Park here, and a short ski on FS 522 will take you to Freidlein Prairie Tank, a small pond on the left side of the road. To reach the upper open meadow of Freidlein Prairie, continue beyond Freidlein Prairie Tank and ski straight uphill for a mile. The climb is gradual and takes you through beautiful groves of aspen. Unobstructed views of the snow-shrouded Agassiz and Fremont peaks are stunning. To the south, the vista sweeps down toward Flagstaff and beyond to Mormon Mountain and the upper rim country. When the snow is fresh, skiing down from Freidlein Prairie through open groves of aspen is rewarding and well worth the climb.

Options to the Freidlein Prairie tour involve connecting the Snow Bowl Road to Schultz Pass (FS 420) along FS 522. The route is six miles across and can be skied in either direction. Coming from Schultz Pass Road, the tour is predominately downhill from Schultz Pass to the Snow Bowl Road. This optional tour requires a full day.

Freidlein Prairie

Hart Prairie

TERRAIN: **Easier**   TIME: **Half-day**
DISTANCE: **Varies**
MAPS: **USGS—Humphreys Peak, Wing Mountain, White Horse Hills,**
       Kendrick Peak
     USFS—Coconino (Note: Due to the amount of area covered by this
       tour, the map pictured here is a metric map.)

High on the west side of the San Francisco Peaks, a prominent hour-glass shaped meadow pours downward onto an immense prairie draped across the rolling foothills of the mountain. This is Hart Prairie, named after Frank Hart, a sheepman who moved into the area in the late 1800s and was one of the first homesteaders in the area.

The open terrain, reliable snow, and sweeping vistas make Hart Prairie one of the most favored and unique areas for ski touring on the San Francisco Peaks. While there are several popular tours on Hart Prairie, many skiers prefer to ski to the prairie and choose their own route across its open terrain, or spend the day playing on the small rounded hills of the area.

Much of the land on Hart Prairie is forest service land, however, there are a number of private residences in the area. Care should be taken to respect these homes, as some of the cabins are occupied year-round and none of them are open to the general public.

Hart Prairie can be reached from several forest service roads along U.S. 180. Hart Prairie Road (FS 151), North Hart Prairie Road (N FS 151), and the Snow Bowl Road are the only roads to Hart Prairie that offer plowed parking in the winter.

The most popular route is Hart Prairie Road (FS 151), which begins three miles north of the Snow Bowl Road (approximately ten miles from Flagstaff). Hart Prairie Road climbs two and a half miles from U.S. 180 where it meets the edge of the prairie; from there, it crosses over and rejoins the highway at North Hart Prairie Road, ten miles away.

A long and scenic tour can be made by skiing the Hart Prairie Road from highway to highway. The tour passes west of Fern Mountain and east of the Hochderffer Hills, across open prairie and through beautiful aspen forests. It is best to arrange a car shuttle from one end to the other.

Another popular tour can be made by skiing one and a half miles up Hart Prairie from FS 151 to the Snow Bowl downhill ski area, and then enjoying the long gentle descent all the way back to U.S. 180. The complete tour up and back is eight miles. Care must be taken on the descent not to miss FS 151 where it leaves the prairie.

The tour around the base of Fern Mountain, the prominent, rounded cinder cone due north of where FS 151 meets the prairie, is good for a moderate day's ski. This tour covers about eight miles. Closer access to the Fern Mountain area is from FS 794, six miles past FS 151, although plowed parking is not usually available.

The Bismark Lake tour begins at North FS 151 and leads five miles to FS 627, which winds one and a half miles up to Bismark Lake. Another half-mile up the road is Lew Tank; from there a long gradual downhill run will bring you back to FS 151 by Fern Mountain.

In 1892 the Grand Canyon Stage Line Company began traversing the rugged road from Flagstaff to the Grand Canyon. The stage would leave Flagstaff in the morning and run through Fort Valley. From there, the route led through the forest until joining the side of Walker Lake and eventually the Grand Canyon. The round trip took two days and cost twenty dollars. Portions of the stage route can be found about a mile up the Hart Prairie Road. Marked on the topo map as a jeep trail, the narrow road works down toward Taylor Spring. From there, it follows the gas pipeline until joining Roundtree Road, a mile east of U.S. 180. From here, follow Roundtree Road to U.S. 180 or follow the gas pipeline to the Snow Bowl Road and then to U.S. 180 at the Snow Bowl parking area.

Touring on prairies at the base of the San Francisco Peaks

Hart Prairie (metric)

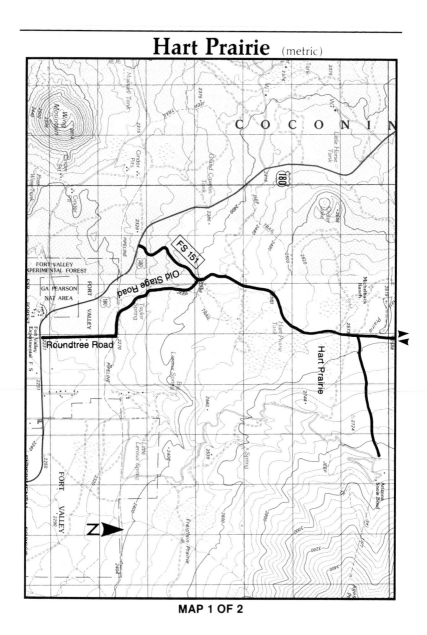

MAP 1 OF 2

Hart Prairie (metric)

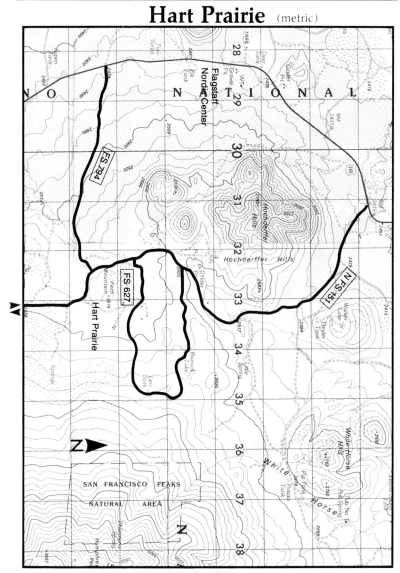

MAP 2 OF 2

Wing Mountain

TERRAIN: **More Difficult**   TIME: **Half-day**
DISTANCE: **7.5 miles**
MAPS: **USGS—Wing Mountain**
     USFS—Coconino

The Wing Mountain area holds some of the most reliable conditions and varied touring terrain accessible via U.S. 180; the terrain is excellent for skiers of all abilities, from beginner to advanced.

In the mid-1800s John Young, son of Mormon leader Brigham Young, moved into the area now known as Ft. Valley. There he established a tent camp for tie cutters working for the Atlantic and Pacific Railroad. As protection against marauding Indians, Ft. Misery was built, its name later changing to Ft. Moroni after the Mormon patron saint. When the A-1 Cattle Company later took possession of the fort, Ellis Wainright, owner of the St. Louis Brewery, worked as general manager. The large cinder cone at the west end of Ft. Valley became known as Wainright Mountain. Later, the name changed to Wing Mountain, coming from a "tinhorn gambler sport" who frequented the fort and local tavern.

Wing Mountain stands among several large cinder cones dotting the way between Flagstaff and Kendrick Peak, west of U.S. 180. Like many of the cinder cones around the base of the San Francisco Peaks, Wing Mountain's summit still forms a small crater. Its accessibility, moderate terrain, and snow-holding ability make it one of the more popular areas in the Flagstaff region for skiers of all abilities. Several large cinder pits circle the parking area, creating perfect practice slopes for downhill technique.

To get to Wing Mountain, drive north on U.S. 180 three miles past the Snow Bowl Road. Wing Mountain Road (FS 222) is on the left just fifty yards past the Hart Prairie Road turnoff (FS 151). Plowed parking is a quarter of a mile down 222.

In 1980 the forest service designated Wing Mountain a cross-country skiing area by establishing several marked trails and restricting motorized vehicles. Of the marked trails in the Wing Mountain area, the most popular one follows forest service roads around Wing Mountain's base. For several years this tour has been the route of the Arizona Citizen's Cup, an annual ten- and thirty-kilometer cross-country ski race, first held in 1974. Although the tour follows mostly gentle terrain, there are a few uphills and a long downhill that warrants the More Difficult rating.

From the parking area, ski to the north of the nearby cinder pits and follow the gas pipeline road to the west. Continue past Maxwell Spring to where FS 222A begins a gradual climb to the south. Bearing left on FS 519, the tour climbs onto the southern shoulder of Wing Mountain, offering a tremendous view of the San Francisco Peaks. Soon, the trail begins its descent toward the intersection with FS 222. Turn left here and follow the road about a mile back to the parking area.

Wing Mountain

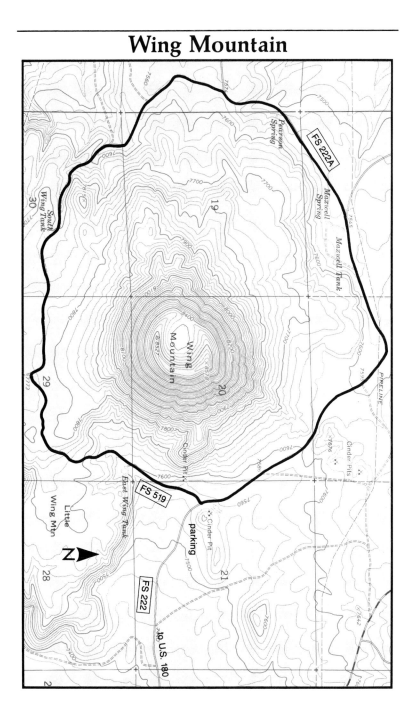

Lava River Cave

TERRAIN: **Easier**   TIME: **Half-day**
DISTANCE: **4.5 miles** one way
MAPS: **USGS—Wing Mountain**
      USFS—Coconino

One of the many interesting phenomena associated with volcanic eruptions is the formation of lava tubes. As the surface of an advancing lava flow cools, the interior may still advance with the weight of the erupting lava behind it. To accommodate the liquid interior, a drainage system develops within the flow, evacuating the molten lava river. As the flow eventually solidifies, these fossilized drain pipes of basalt are left behind, a vestige of the movement of lava through the area, 1.5 million years ago.

Although their original discovery date is uncertain, they were likely used by the Indians of the area for centuries. Later, local ranchers used the caves as a source of ice.

Four miles north of the Wing Mountain Road, approximately fourteen miles out U.S.180, FS 245 takes off to the west through the forest past Aspen Tank. In less than two miles, FS 245 enters a large open area, where Kendrick Mountain comes into view. The road swings north and west, and in another mile, joins FS 171. Turning left, you will meet FS 171B in one mile. This is the turnoff to the Lava River Caves, half a mile to the east. Return via the same route.

Although a popular spot in the summer, the one-mile-deep Lava River Caves seldom have visitors in the winter. A large circular wall marks the cave entrance. Walking over the snow-covered rubble can be awkward. A sign warns "ENTER CAVES AT OWN RISK," good advice, since it is fairly cold and icy inside, and you are a long way from any immediate help. Make sure you bring extra warm clothing for exploring the caves and carry several reliable sources of light.

Lava River Cave

Hochderffer Hills

TERRAIN: **More Difficult**   TIME: **Half-day**
DISTANCE: **2.5 miles** one way
MAPS: **USGS—Wing Mountain, Kendrick Peak, Humphreys Peak**
          USFS—Coconino

In 1887 Frank Hochderffer and his family drove their dusty covered wagon into the freshly burnt town of Flagstaff. Although they were en route to California, the Hochderffer family halted their journey to set up a brick factory and help restore the town.

The Hochderffers became prominent citizens in Flagstaff's pioneer history. Frank's son George spent his life in the area as a farmer, rancher, town marshall, and soldier. The family homesteaded an area at the foot of the hills northwest of Hart Prairie, which now bears their name. George's Summit Ranch once rested by Little Spring near Fern Mountain. When the government acquired the lands in that area, several of the old homesteads were burnt down, thus erasing some vestiges of Flagstaff's pioneer history.

There are several routes into the Hochderffer Hills; the most popular and shortest public route begins approximately fifteen miles from Flagstaff on FS 151E, across from the Deer Tanks (FS 193). Parking is available a tenth of a mile past FS 193 on the west side of the highway. From here, return to FS 193, cross the highway to the east and follow a road for one mile until it joins FS 151E (see forest service map). Heading uphill on FS 151E leads to the central meadow of the Hochderffer Hills. Continue along the road until reaching the small valley that overlooks Hart Prairie and the San Francisco Peaks. This is the apex of the tour and the top of the ski trails for the Flagstaff Nordic Center. As a fee is required for using the nordic center trails, it is best to keep to the side of the tracks as much as possible. (Another and shorter route into the Hochderffer Hills uses their trail system and begins at the Flagstaff Nordic Center rental shop.)

For a better view and some good downhill practice, climb the hill to the west and continue into the basin beyond. The sparse trees, sloped terrain, and spectacular views make this a worthwhile touring area for cutting some graceful telemark turns, especially after a fresh snowfall. Return via the same route.

Hochderffer Hills

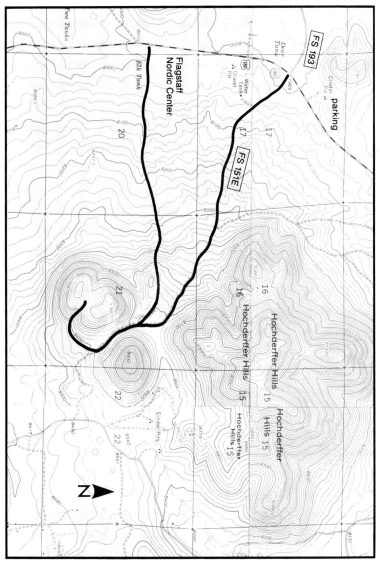

Skier views San Francisco Peaks from the Hochderffer Hills

Kendrick Peak

TERRAIN: **More Difficult**   TIME: **Multiday**
DISTANCE: **10 miles** one way
MAPS: **USGS—Kendrick Peak, Wing Mountain**
      USFS—Coconino, South Kaibab

North of Wing Mountain along U.S. 180 stands Kendrick Peak, a prominent feature of the volcanic skyline. Although dwarfed by the neighboring San Francisco Peaks, Kendrick rises to a lofty 10,418 feet and is the highest volcano of the San Francisco Peaks Volcanic Field, aside from, of course, the peaks themselves.

When Captain Lorenzo Sitgreaves passed through the area, scouting a western route to California in 1851, several geographic features were named for members of his expedition. Across Government Prairie from Sitgreaves Mountain stands the peak named for his scout and military escort, Major Henry L. Kendrick.

The tour to the top of Kendrick Peak leads to a small cabin, once used as the summer home for fire lookouts. The cabin is no longer in service, but is kept open throughout the year for visitor use. Inside, rustic accommodations include a woodstove and two cots, a rewarding camp for a winter night.

The tour to the top of Kendrick Peak begins on the Deer Tank Road (FS 193) about fifteen miles north of Flagstaff. Parking is available a tenth of a mile past the FS 193 turnoff. From here, return to FS 193, and follow it for three miles to FS 171. Follow FS 171 for another two miles west to the trailhead on FS 171A. The four-mile trail switchbacks up 2,400 feet on the peak's south side. At the top, the trail passes through an open meadow to the cabin. Skiing around on Kendrick's summit and visiting the lookout tower are tremendous ways to get a feel for the lay of the land surrounding the San Francisco Peaks.

Allow one long day or two short ones for the climb up. Carry plenty of water, warm clothes, and matches. The return down the trail can be tricky on skis with a pack. For a more adventurous descent, it is possible to ski down Kendrick's north side, after some scouting.

Although this tour is described as a multiday trip, the road leading to the base of Kendrick Peak offers excellent Easier touring terrain.

Kendrick Peak

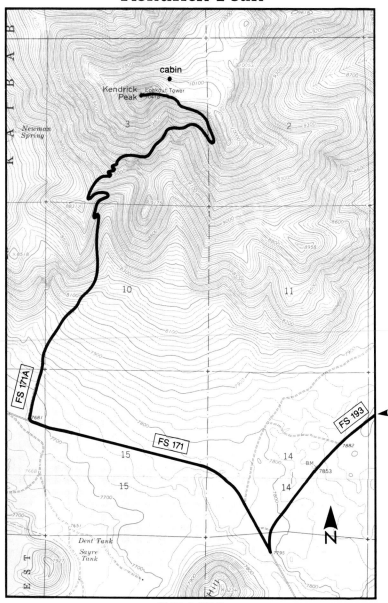

MAP 2 OF 2

Kendrick Peak

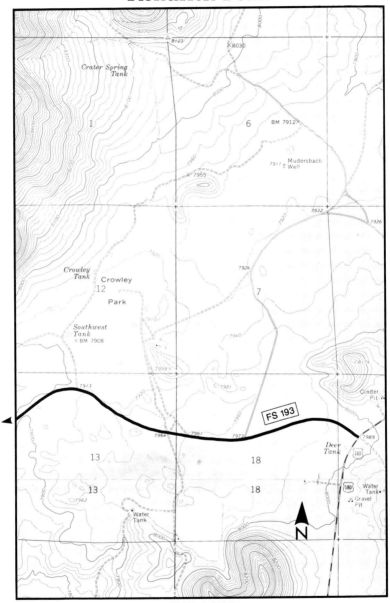

MAP 1 OF 2

Walker Lake

TERRAIN: **More Difficult**   TIME: **Half-day**
DISTANCE: **5 miles**
MAPS: **USGS—White Horse Hills, Kendrick Peak**
     USFS—Coconino

Many of the cinder cones in the San Francisco Peaks Volcanic Field hide open craters containing small lakes on their summits. Walker Lake is a classic example and is easily accessible for the ski tourer. Originally called Blowout Tank by local cattlemen, Walker Lake was probably named for Ace Walker, a young Mormon bullwhacker who drove freight to Lees Ferry on the Colorado River.

About seventeen miles north of Flagstaff on U.S. 180, just south of the open plains of Kendrick Park, is the North Hart Prairie Road (FS 151). Parking is available here or a quarter of a mile past FS 151 at a major left-hand curve. From here, ski one and a half miles on FS 151 through the aspens to a left-hand junction with FS 418. Down this road a short way is another road branching north toward the Walker Lake cinder cone. Dirt bars built as vehicle deterrents punctuate the road to Walker Lake's cone rim, which make the descent exciting and the tour rating intermediate.

After cresting the rim, you ski down to the quiet expanse of Walker Lake. Touring around the lake or crossing its surface (BEWARE OF THIN ICE) is a good way to enjoy the lake's serenity. A return-trip option is to drop through the trees on the cone's north side and return through the forest to the west, back to FS 151.

White Horse Hills

TERRAIN: **More Difficult**   TIME: **Full day**
DISTANCE: **5 miles** one way
MAPS: **USGS—White Horse Hills, Kendrick Peak**
     USFS—Coconino

At the base of the long ridge that drops off the north side of Humphreys Peak lies a small cluster of domes called the White Horse Hills. In 1888 Frank Hochderffer purchased several Indian ponies that roamed the flanks of these hills east of his homestead. One pony in particular, "a pinto with about as much dun color as white," took to the area and spent the better part of the next twenty years on the hills. Local cowboys and settlers often called the area the White Horse Hills in reference to the pony.

Following the directions to Walker Lake (see previous tour), continue on FS

Walker Lake/White Horse Hills

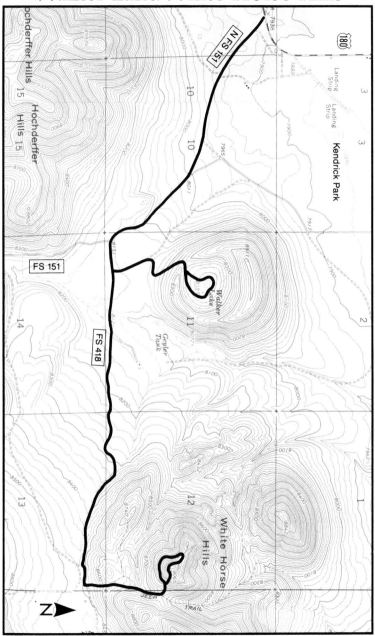

418 past the Walker Lake road for two miles. The road passes along the edge of a large field and around the south side of the White Horse Hills. There are several private residences in the area; care should be taken not to disturb them.

Just past the junction with FS 418B, the road meets the closed jeep road that climbs into the White Horse Hills. A short distance up the road, the terrain levels then begins to drop down the hills' north side. From this saddle, another road winds steeply to the summit of the White Horse Hills. From here, exhilarating views of the peaks and surrounding country can be seen.

Although it's easiest to return via the same route, another possibility is to continue north on the road from the saddle and work back through the forests to the west. This route involves some cross-country navigation and takes you through the major burn north of Walker Lake to FS 514A, which leads back to the North Hart Prairie Road (FS 151).

Saddle Mountain

TERRAIN: **More Difficult**   TIME: **Half-day**
DISTANCE: **2.5 miles** one way
MAPS: **USGS—White Horse Hills, Kendrick Peak**
      USFS—Coconino

Saddle Mountain lies due north of the White Horse Hills and the San Francisco Peaks. Perched above the long pinyon-juniper plateau that drops toward the Grand Canyon, Saddle Mountain offers tremendous views north to the North Rim and east into the Little Colorado Basin. Spectacular views to the south are dominated by the cones and volcanoes of the San Francisco Peaks Volcanic Field.

Within a mile past the North Hart Prairie road turnoff (FS 151), and about twenty miles north of Flagstaff, U.S. 180 crosses the broad expanse of Kendrick Park. In the northeast corner of the park stands the rounded cinder cone of Saddle Mountain. Across Kendrick Park on its northern edge there is a rest area on the left, which is often plowed for parking. To ski to Saddle Mountain, cross U.S. 180.

There are two options to skiing up Saddle Mountain. One is to follow the fence across from the parking area east to the north side of Saddle Mountain. Continue around the base of Saddle Mountain until joining FS 550A, which climbs to the summit. Another option is to follow the fence across from the parking area east for one mile, then ski cross country toward the base of Saddle Mountain's west side. From there, ski up a hidden drainage toward the southern end of the mountain until reaching FS 550A, which continues toward the top.

The open summit of Saddle Mountain is a good break spot. Remains of an old lookout tower lie buried beneath the snow. Descent is easiest via the route up, although it is possible, with good snow conditions, to descend the northeast side. The open west side can be excellent for telemark skiing after a storm.

Saddle Mountain

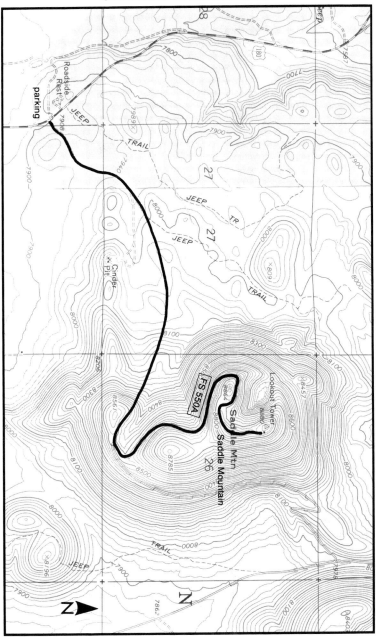

SAN FRANCISCO PEAKS EAST

U.S. Highway 89

Highway 89 north from Flagstaff climbs through the cinder cones and volcanic outwash of the San Francisco Peaks' east side. It is from this side that you can climb into the interior basins of the peaks. These basins are the remains of the inner caldera of the San Francisco Peaks volcano, whose eastern rim collapsed and opened up within the last two million years.

This is some of the most remote terrain of the San Francisco Peaks. Tours into this region offer good opportunities for the ski mountaineer as well as the intermediate tourer. The elevation and exposure of the high terrain in this area give it the longest snow season in the state.

Although it is occasionally possible to ski in other areas along U.S. 89—such as the burn area east of Mt. Elden or near Sunset Crater and O'Leary Peak—the snow in these areas is often too sparse for good skiing; hence these areas are not discussed in this guidebook. As such, all the tours in this section climb into the Inner Basin and onto the north side of the peaks. These tours are all reached by the Lockett Meadow Road (FS 552), approximately seventeen miles north of Flagstaff. Due to distance and elevation, these tours require full days or overnight camping, depending on conditions.

Drying out sleeping bags on a winter camping trip

Lockett Meadow

TERRAIN: **More Difficult**   TIME: **Full day**
DISTANCE: **4.5 miles** one way
MAPS: **USGS—O'Leary Peak, Sunset Crater West, Humphreys Peak**
      USFS—Coconino

Lockett Meadow, the small meadow that serves as the portal to the Inner Basin of the San Francisco Peaks, is named for Henry Claiborne Lockett, who arrived in Flagstaff by mule team from Kansas in 1881. As a farmer, sheepman, and member of the Territorial Senate, Lockett is a prominent figure in Flagstaff history. Lockett Meadow, Road, and Spring all bear his name.

The small meadow, often a favorite picnic spot during the summer months, lies still and serene under white snows of winter. From the meadow you can see far into the upper reaches of the Inner Basin and the summits of Fremont and Agassiz peaks. Evidence of glaciation—the u-shaped valley and large morraines—is now covered by blankets of aspen, spruce, and fir that quietly flank the meadow and the valley above.

Just over seventeen miles from Flagstaff, on north U.S. 89, FS 552 heads west through a fence near the base of a partially excavated cinder cone. It is usually possible to ski from here, although in leaner winters or spring, you can drive in farther. Roughly a mile up the road, FS 552 turns north and begins its long climb around the flanks of Sugarloaf Mountain. Driving this ascent is recommended only under lean snow conditions.

Representing one of the youngest episodes of vulcanism in the area, this rounded dome formed about 220,000 years ago as an explosion of steam, caused as rising magma contacted undergound water. The resulting depression and ring of debris was then filled by viscous silicic lava, whose texture gives Sugarloaf Mountain its name.

Although a substantial tour in its own right, the trip to Lockett Meadow serves as a gateway to longer tours higher up in the San Francisco Peaks. While it is possible to do these tours in a day, depending on snow and road conditions, they are excellent for overnight winter camping trips. From a base camp in Lockett Meadow, day trips into the upper valleys and even the summit peaks are possible.

Inner Basin

TERRAIN: **More Difficult**   TIME: **Full day or Multiday**
DISTANCE: **4 miles** from Lockett Meadow
MAPS: **USGS—Humphreys Peak, Sunset Crater West**
     USFS—Coconino

From Lockett Meadow (see previous tour), a one-and-a-half-mile climb up FS 552 (not shown on USGS topo map) leads to several cabins at a small crossroad. These cabins serve as the collection sight for Flagstaff's water supply. From here, water drops around the peaks' south side to two large reservoirs at the base of Shultz Pass Road. These cabins are not for public use and should not be disturbed. Also, because the terrain above is the source of Flagstaff's watershed, camping is not permitted above this point (check with Coconino National Forest for camping areas on San Francisco Peaks).

Continue up FS 552C two miles to the open glaciated benches of the Inner Basin. Much of the steep, open terrain above has been cleared by avalanches. Although infrequent, avalanches are a very real part of ski touring on the peaks, and a good knowledge of avalanche safety is important before attempting to ski in avalanche terrain (see pages 10–12).

High to the left, the long avalanche chute of Telemark Path sweeps down from the summit of Fremont Peak. Across this face winds the Weatherford Toll Road that once brought tourists by wagon and car to the summit ridges of the San Francisco Peaks in the 1930s and '40s. To the west, Agassiz Peak, second highest of the summits, dominates the skyline. The north side of the valley is flanked by the Secondary Core Ridge, little brother to the prominent and rocky Core Ridge that descends to the east from the Agassiz-Humphreys ridge and divides the interior valley of the peaks.

Due to its elevation and exposure, conditions in the Inner Basin are often excellent for skiing when snow elsewhere is melting or gone. In fact, it is often possible to ski here well into the spring and early summer.

Bear Paw Spring

TERRAIN: **More Difficult**   TIME: **Full day or Multiday**
DISTANCE: **3 miles** from Lockett Meadow
MAPS: **USGS—Humphreys Peak, Sunset Crater West**
  USFS—Coconino

A short distance beyond the watershed cabins (see previous tour), a road bears right and leads one mile to the north side of the Core Ridge. This is the valley of Bear Paw Spring, Flagstaff Spring, and the tangent Beard and Dunham canyons, which drain the steep, cliff-banded east face of Humphreys Peak. It was on this side of the mountain in 1973, that an immense avalanche broke loose down Dunham Canyon, overflowed the canyon boundaries, and snapped tall spruce and fir trees in half. Tree-ring dating indicates this was one of the largest avalanches of the previous one hundred years and *the* largest of fourteen releases over the past fifty years.

From Bear Paw Spring it is possible to continue up canyon another mile to Flagstaff Spring, although the terrain gets steeper as you go up. Return via the same route.

Abineau Canyon

TERRAIN: **More Difficult**   TIME: **Full day or Multiday**
DISTANCE: **7 miles** from Lockett Meadow
MAPS: **USGS—Humphreys Peak, Sunset Crater West**
  USFS—Coconino

Gradually working its way upward around the north side of the peaks, FS 146 dead-ends in Abineau Canyon at the base of three prominent chutes on the north slope of Humphreys Peak. The five-mile road turns north at the watershed cabins above Lockett Meadow and follows a very gradual grade with stunning views of the country to the east and north. The northernmost and most prominent of the three chutes is Crossfire Path. As the name implies, two avalanche runs cross halfway down and run to the bottom of the canyon below. In an interesting display of force, one avalanche crossed its runout zone and ran up the canyon wall on the far side—certainly a testimony to the velocity and momentum of an avalanche.

The return to the watershed cabins comfortably drops along the road, making for a relaxing return to camp or the highway.

Lockett Meadow, Inner Basin, . . .

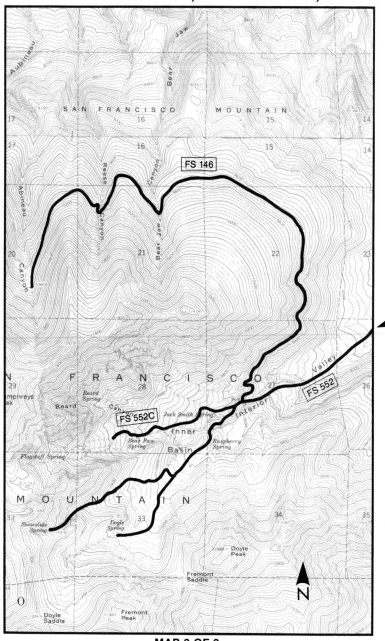

MAP 2 OF 2

...Bear Paw Spring, Abineau Canyon

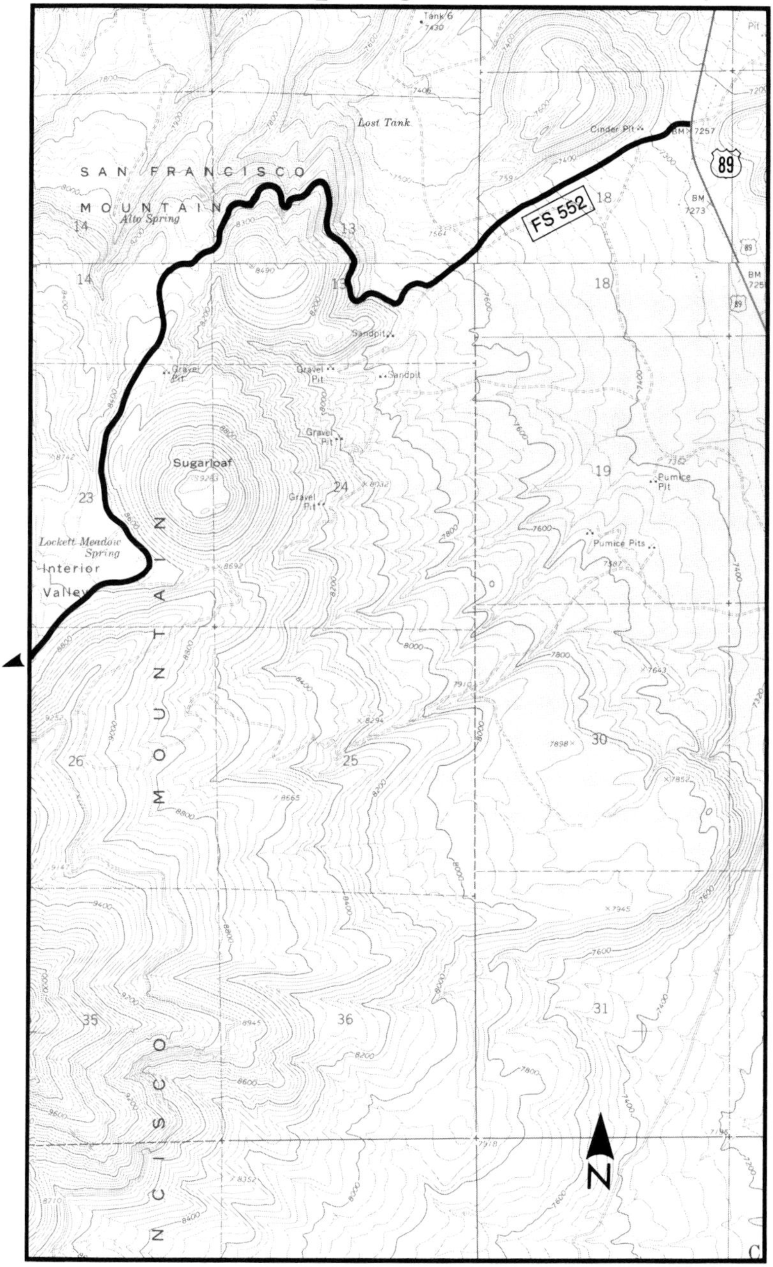

MAP 1 OF 2

SAN FRANCISCO PEAKS

Tours from the Top

The summits of the San Francisco Peaks can be reached from most sides of the mountain. The highest road access during the winter months is the Snow Bowl Road, which climbs eight miles from U.S. 180 to the upper reaches of Hart Prairie (9,500 feet). Often chains or four-wheel drive are required by the county for vehicles using the road.

From the parking lot at Snow Bowl, there are several ways to reach the summit ridge. The easiest and most expensive option is, of course, to purchase a lift ticket and ride the number one chair to the 11,600-foot level on Agassiz Peak's west ridge. As yet, the Snow Bowl does not offer tickets on a per-ride basis.

One skiing option involves a two- to three-hour ski up the ski area slopes. From the top of the area, work up and north toward the summit ridge below Mt. Agassiz. When skiing up the ski area, it is important to stay to the sides of the runs and out of the way of the alpine skiers. This protects you as well as your ability to have access to the groomed slopes in the future.

In 1985 the forest service constructed a foot trail to the saddle between Agassiz and Humphreys peaks. The trail begins on the north side of Hart Prairie, about halfway up the ski run. Taking off through the forest, the trail winds up for three and a half miles until it breaks out above treeline and lands on the saddle above Flagstaff Spring. Although the trail is certainly more quiet and less crowded than the ski slopes, it is a little hard to follow in places.

The tours that follow describe several routes up and over the summits of the San Francisco Peaks. Because the Snow Bowl Road usually serves as a starting point, tour distances are measured from the upper parking lot by the Agassiz Lodge at the ski area. Whether climbing the peaks from Snow Bowl or a more backcountry route, always carry necessary maps. Furthermore, allow more time than distance may indicate, as terrain, elevation, and a circuitous or zig-zagging route add to what may seem a simple, straightforward line.

Lenticular clouds building over north side of Humphreys Peak

Humphreys Peak

TERRAIN: **More Difficult** TIME: **Full day**
DISTANCE: **6 miles**
MAPS: **USGS—Humphreys Peak**
   USFS—Coconino

The tour to Humphreys Peak (12,633 feet), Arizona's highest point, gives one of the most unique and satisfying views in the area and is suprisingly accessible. Following the forest service trail from Hart Prairie, or skiing to the top of the number one chair at the ski area, traverse north toward the major saddle between Agassiz and Humphreys peaks. From there, follow the ridge north to the summit. Return via the same route.

While this tour follows a fairly straightforward route, wind and bad weather can make it unforgiving. More than once tourers have died on the peaks due to poor preparation and experience. Strong winds scour the ridges, leaving a hard-to-ski snowpack as well as large, precarious cornices overhanging steep avalanche chutes. Often it is easier to walk than to ski along the summit ridge. Sudden storms limit visibility and can be disorienting.

Telemarking in fresh snow

Humphreys Peak

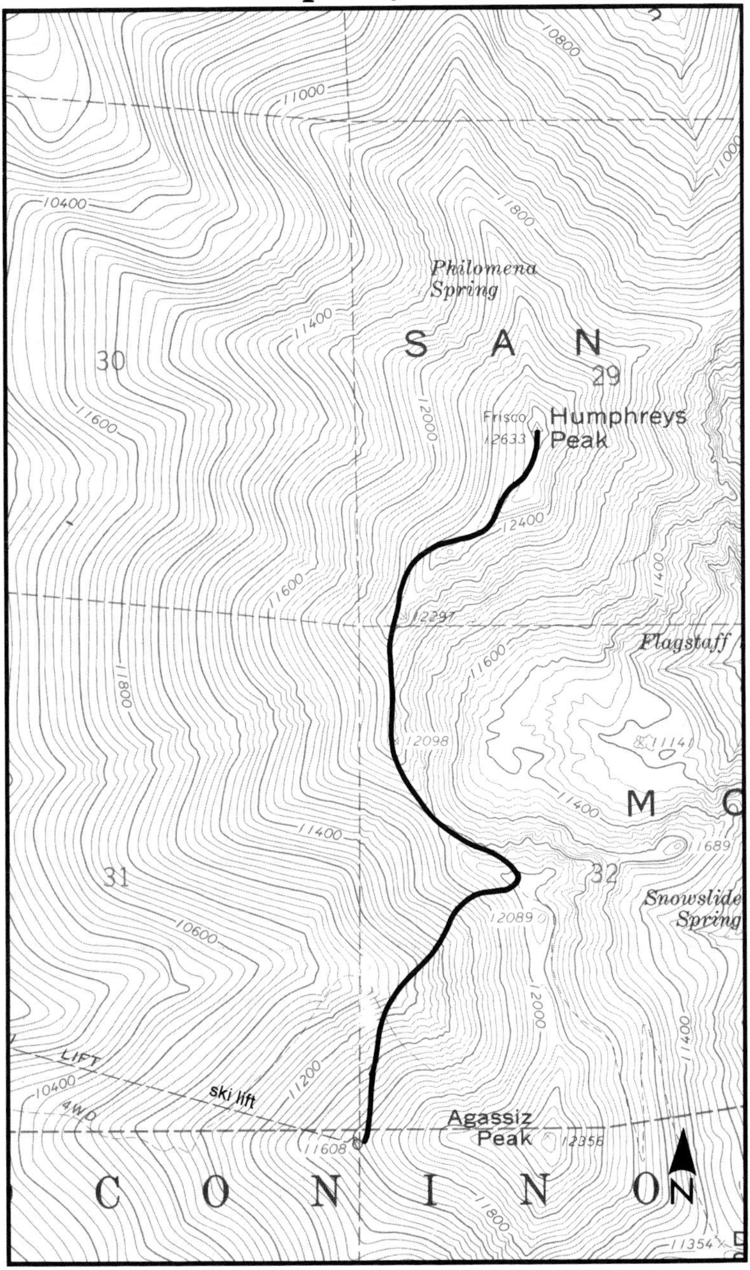

Philomena Spring

S A N

Frisco Humphreys Peak

Flagstaff

M C

Snowslide Spring

Agassiz Peak

C O N I N O N

South Side

TERRAIN: **Most Difficult**   TIME: **Full day**
DISTANCE: **5 miles** one way
MAPS: **USGS—Humphreys Peak**
     USFS—Coconino

Skiing the south side of Agassiz Peak is one of the most accessible backcountry trips off the San Francisco Peaks and offers tremendous views of Flagstaff and the rim country to the south. With a southern exposure, this tour is best with a fresh layer of snow on a good base. Choose a day when the trees are frosted white from the peaks' base to their summits.

From the parking lot at the Snow Bowl, ski up to the top of chair number one on Agassiz Peak. From there, contour around to the south for a quarter- to a half-mile. This traverse leads across several chutes that can slide with a good snow load; take extreme care when crossing any of these open areas on the peaks. Several inviting routes soon come into view, and most tend to funnel into the prominent drainage ahead. Pick one that looks good and head down and left toward the drainage. Because the lower parts of the drainage become thick with trees, cut right onto a shoulder that leads down through open aspen forests to the Freidlein Prairie Road (see Freidlein Prairie Tour). Head west (right) on FS 522 until you reach Snow Bowl Road. If the snow is adequate, it is possible to ski beside the road down to U.S. 180.

Because this tour eventually leads back to Snow Bowl Road where it junctions with FS 522, it is possible to leave a car here or hitchhike up or down Snow Bowl Road to your vehicle.

South Side

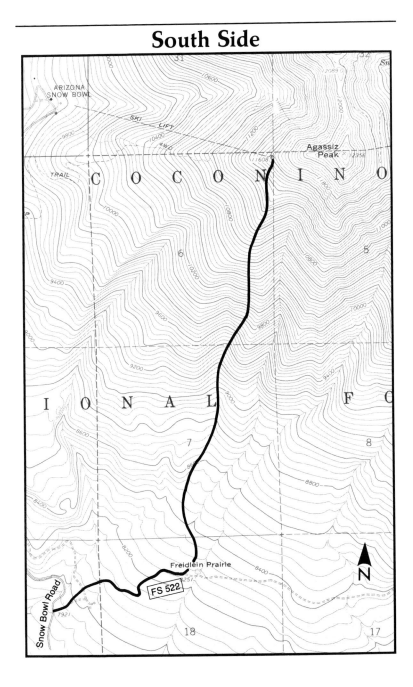

Inner Basin/Snowslide Spring

TERRAIN: **Most Difficult**   TIME: **Full day**
DISTANCE: **12 miles** one way
MAPS: **USGS—Humphreys Peak, Sunset Crater West, O'Leary Peak
USFS—Coconino**

The trip down the Inner Basin is one of the most popular tours over the mountain. Despite its relative popularity, the Inner Basin Tour remains an uncrowded ski mountaineering trip, yet its remoteness adds an element of seriousness.

When snow begins to melt elsewhere on the mountain, the slopes of the Inner Basin are often still fresh and powdery. Spring skiing in the upper bowls of the Inner Basin continues long after the rest of the mountain is bare.

The shuttle for this tour involves leaving a vehicle where FS 552 meets U.S. 89, depending on conditions (see Lockett Meadow Tour). Arrange your shuttle early, as the tour up and over the Inner Basin requires a full day.

Follow the forest service trail, or ski to the top of the number one chair, and work your way over to the large saddle to the north of Agassiz Peak. The slope below splits into the drainages of Snowslide Spring to the north and Doyle Spring to the south through the trees. Either way, the descent is exhilarating, steep, and fast.

As the name implies, Snowslide Spring is just that, an avalanche chute. In 1973, along with Dunham Canyon to the north, Snowslide ran to ground and plunged through the trees well into the canyon below. The drainages below are flanked by glacial remains from Pleistocene times, over 20,000 years ago. Following the drainages past the watershed cabins, FS 552 makes a speedy descent into Lockett Meadow and continues around Sugarloaf Mountain to U.S. 89.

Inner Basin/Snowslide Spring

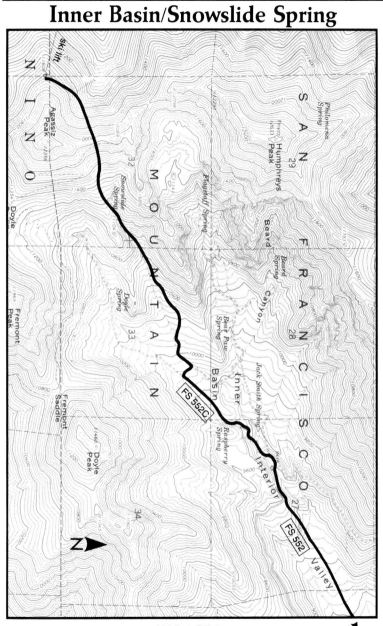

MAP 1 OF 2

Inner Basin/Snowslide Spring

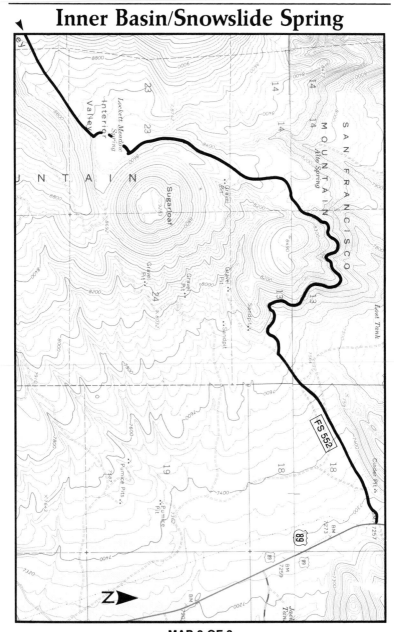

MAP 2 OF 2

SPECIALTY TOURS

There are several tours particular to the San Francisco Peaks that have been completed by local skiers over the years. Besides their uniqueness, these tours are physically demanding and cover a lot of distance. Two of the tours involve vertical-mile descents from the summit of Arizona, Humphreys Peak, and another involves a circumnavigation of the peaks. Several variations and additions to these tours are also possible.

North Side Vertical Mile

TERRAIN: **Most Difficult**   TIME: **Full day**
DISTANCE: **12 miles**
MAPS: **USGS—Humphreys Peak, O'Leary Peak, Sunset Crater West**
       USFS—Coconino

Beginning from the top of Humphreys Peak (see Humphreys Peak Tour), this tour continues down the North Ridge and drops off into the trees in Abineau Canyon. This is extreme avalanche country, so be sure conditions are stable before entering any of the chutes! From Abineau Canyon, follow the road (FS 146) that leads to the watershed cabins and continue on FS 552 through Lockett Meadow and out to U.S. 89, a total drop of 5,413 feet.

It is necessary to have a shuttle vehicle on FS 552 or be picked up there after your tour.

North Side Vertical Mile

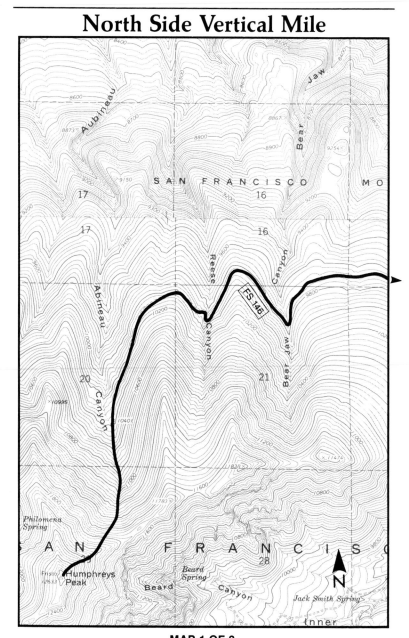

MAP 1 OF 3

North Side Vertical Mile

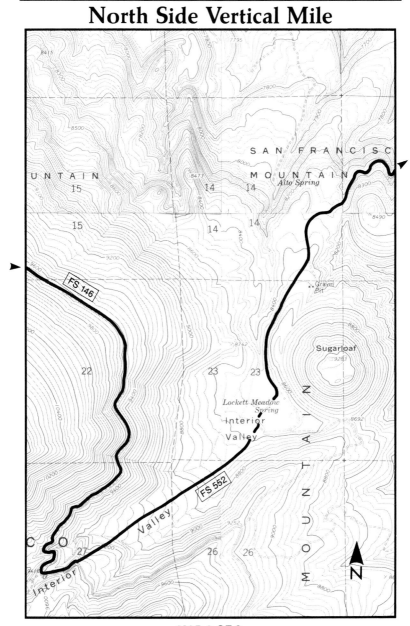

MAP 2 OF 3

North Side Vertical Mile

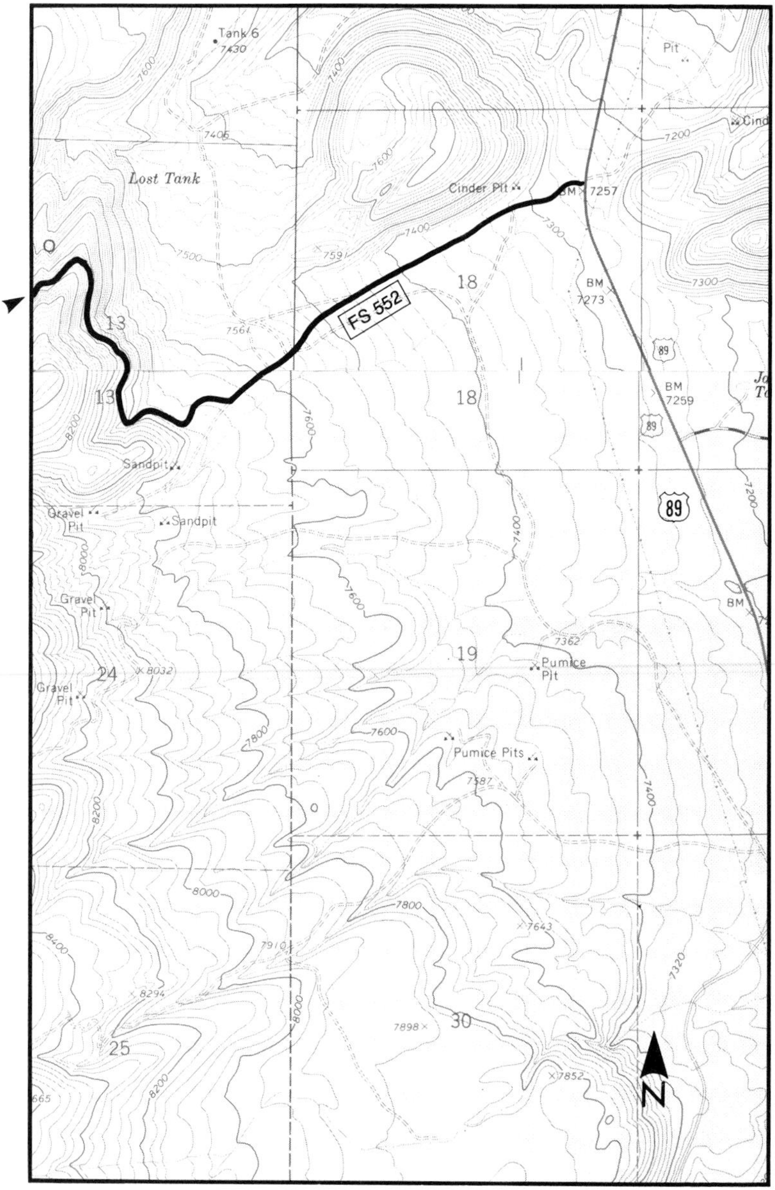

MAP 3 OF 3

West Side Vertical Mile

TERRAIN: **Most Difficult**   TIME: **Full day**
DISTANCE: **12 miles**
MAPS: **USGS—Humphreys Peak**
     USFS—Coconino

From the Humphreys Peak summit (see Humphreys Peak Tour), and with stable snow conditions permitting, ski down the prominent chute on the west side of the peaks. This is known as Allison's Rock Slide, named after a woman who froze here during a winter camping trip in the late '70s. At the bottom of the chute, a thick section of forest eventually drops you onto Hart Prairie. From here, ski south to FS 151 and follow it from Hart Prairie to the old stage route jeep road that leads to Taylor Spring and across the fields to the Snow Bowl Road at U.S. 180, a total drop of 5,292 feet. For more details on the runout, see Hart Prairie.

Peaks Circle Tour

TERRAIN: **More Difficult**   TIME: **Multiday**
DISTANCE: **42 miles**
MAPS: **USGS—Humphreys Peak, Sunset Crater West**
     USFS—Coconino (Note: Due to the amount of area covered by this tour, the map pictured is a metric map.)

From the Snow Bowl Road at U.S. 180, ski along the gas pipeline past Taylor Spring to Hart Prairie and follow FS 151 across the prairie to FS 418B. This road joins FS 418 at the White Horse Hills. Ski east to Reese Tanks, then using map, compass, and some wit, climb the drainage to Abineau Canyon. From here, a long downhill descent follows FS 146 past the watershed cabins on FS 552 and continues around the peaks to Shultz Pass. A short climb on FS 522 leads across Freidlein Prairie to the Snow Bowl Road, which can be followed back to U.S. 180.

There are several roads along the way that access U.S. 180 and U.S. 89. The trip can take from three to five days with packs depending on conditions and side-tour diversions.

West Side Vertical Mile

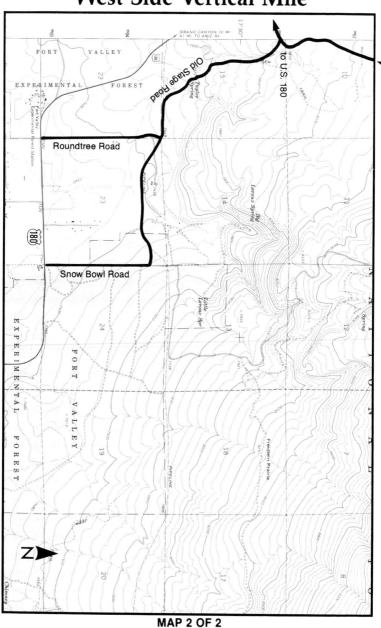

MAP 2 OF 2

West Side Vertical Mile

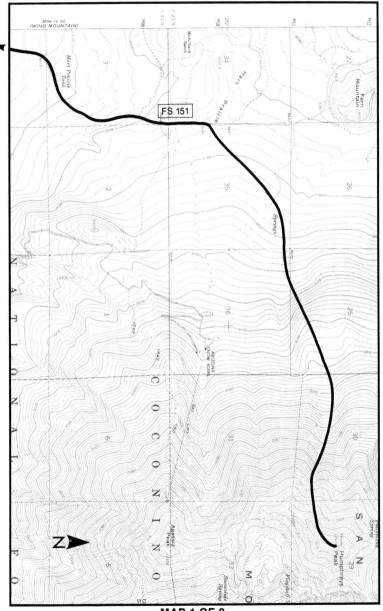

FS 151

MAP 1 OF 2

Peaks Circle Tour (metric)

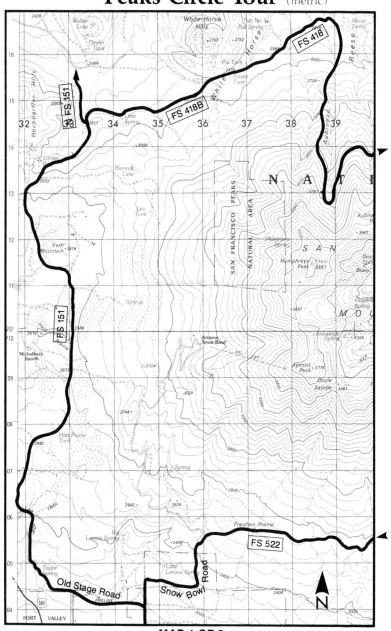

MAP 1 OF 2

Peaks Circle Tour (metric)

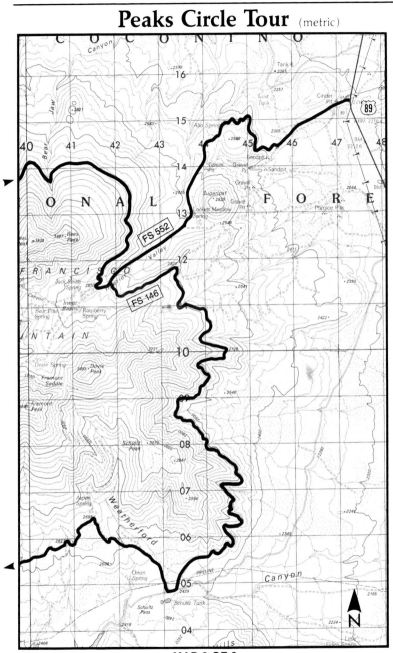

MAP 2 OF 2

Creek near Mormon Mountain

MORMON LAKE/MOUNTAIN

Mormon Lake

TERRAIN: **Easier to More Difficult** TIME: **Short to Full day**
DISTANCE: **Variable**
MAPS: **USGS—Mormon Mountain, Mormon Lake**
   USFS—Coconino

A dairy farm was the goal of the Mormon wagon train that rolled into the large, marshy valley south of Flagstaff in 1878. However, as drainage from the spring-fed grazing fields became poor, the fields flooded to form the broad, shallow lake known as Mormon Lake. The filling of Mormon Lake was the end of the dairy business there, and in the years to come, the dairy became a ranch and later a lodge and ski-touring center.

The largest natural lake in Coconino County, Mormon Lake stretches for three miles across the valley, 1,500 feet below the summit of Mormon Mountain, the smallest major volcano of the San Francisco Peaks Volcanic Field.

Besides its rich cultural history, Mormon Lake has a cross-country ski history that stretches back to the 1930s when skis were a necessity for working around the lodge in the winter months. This was the sight of Gordan Evans's and Charley Simpson's epic journey to Flagstaff on skis.

Mormon Lake is the home of some of the first established cross-country ski trails in the state. Today, two sets of ski trails snake through the forest at the base of Mormon Mountain: those of the Mormon Lake Lodge and the Montezuma Nordic Center.

One particularly nice meadow lies about a mile north of Montezuma Nordic Center and was the site of several Arizona Cup Races. At the far end of the meadow are remnants of a sawmill that cut railroad ties for the train carrying logs through this area to Flagstaff; the old locomotive now sits idle on the lawn of Southwest Forest Industries.

The elevation of Mormon Lake is similar to Flagstaff, and as a result, the area has a shorter skiing season than the higher elevations of the forest. However, when the snow falls, it's worth trying some of the trails in the area. If you are up for a longer day tour, try the trail to the top of Mormon Mountain that begins in the campground at the Montezuma Nordic Center. A more moderate route to the top can be made up the Antelope Park Road, which crosses the mountain's north side, connecting with a road from Mud Springs that leads to the top. Like many of the major hills in the area, Mormon Mountain's broad summit is the home of several radio and TV towers. This is a good spot for bird's eye views of the San Francisco Peaks and the great expanse of Mormon Lake.

For directions and conditions, consult one of the local touring areas.

Mormon Lake

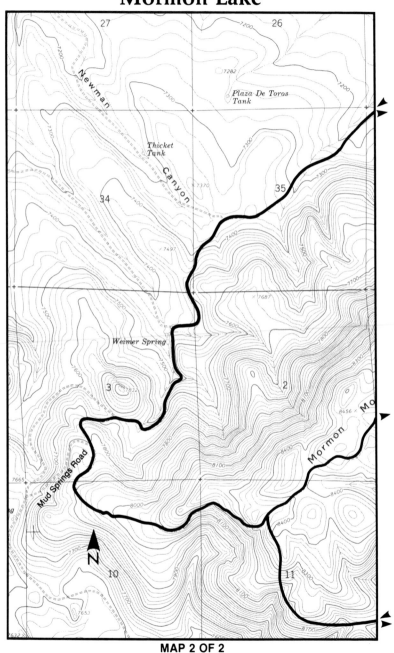

MAP 2 OF 2

Mormon Lake

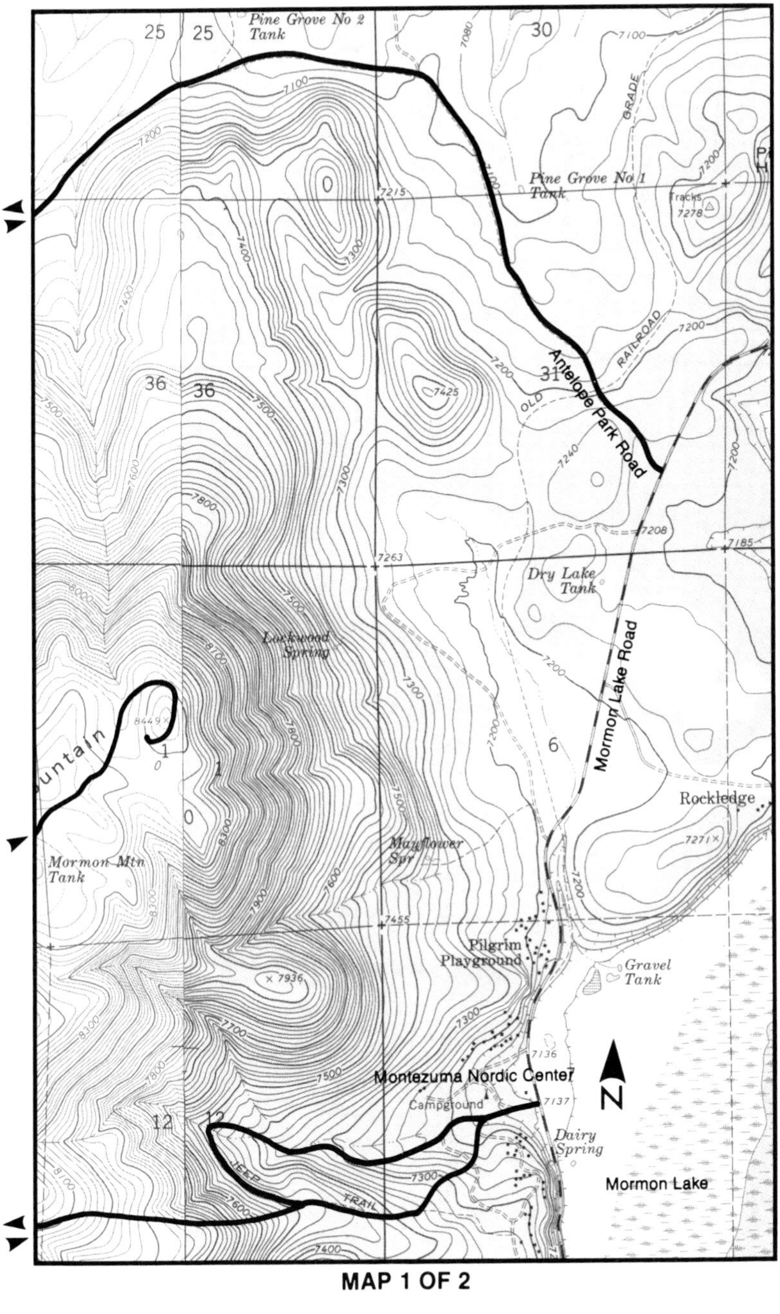

MAP 1 OF 2

Tourer, Bill Williams Mountain

BILL WILLIAMS MOUNTAIN

William Sherley Williams was a classic figure among western frontiersmen. Born in North Carolina in 1787, Bill Williams left home at a young age to live among the Osage tribe. Later, this tall, redheaded man lived his life as a preacher and mountainman, hunting, trapping, and working as a scout for several western survey expeditions. After surviving a severe winter with the Fremont Expedition, Bill Williams died in 1849 at the age of 62 near Blanca Peak in southern Colorado during a skirmish with a local Indian tribe.

The town of Williams, thirty miles west of Flagstaff, lies at the foot of Bill Williams Mountain (9,256 feet). Both town and peak were named in honor of the mountain man by Richard H. Kern, a mapmaker who had worked alongside Bill Williams during the Fremont Expedition. Kern passed through the Williams area in 1851 with the Sitgreaves Survey while scouting a wagon route west for California immigrants.

The Williams area offers many possibilities for the ski tourer. Miles of forest roads wind through the woods south of town toward the head of Sycamore Canyon and are skiable in heavier winters. For nordic downhill practice, the Williams Ski Run is an ideal ski area with moderate terrain, small crowds, and reasonable prices.

For information on snow conditions in the Williams area, contact the Kaibab National Forest Ranger Station in Williams (see reference list page 133).

Ski Jump Tour

TERRAIN: **Easier**   TIME: **Short Day**
DISTANCE: **2 miles**
MAPS: **USGS—Bill Williams Mountain**
       USFS—South Kaibab

On a fall day in 1948, several members of the small but growing Williams Ski Club were working their way along the northern slopes of Bill Williams Mountain. Led by club founder and Williams Ski Run developer Ed Grosbeak, they ended their search and began cutting a narrow swath down through the thick spruce beneath a large rock outcrop. This was the beginning of the Williams Ski Jump, one of the biggest in the country at the time. With the ramp at a forty-five percent grade and the landing at sixty-five percent, this modern facility was equipped to witness record jumps of up to 150 feet. After the ski area was relocated, the ski jump fell out of use and into disrepair; today a stand of young aspen trees reaches skyward as the aspiring youth of Williams once did on their skis.

South of Williams on 4th Street, signs lead to the Williams Ski Run. From the parking area of the Williams Ski Run, FS 106 continues up the valley past the ski area. The road slowly climbs for a mile past a switchback and ends on a long flat bench. This bench was the runout zone for the old ski jump, which loomed above and to the right of a large rock outcrop. This tour is nice for a short break from skiing at the ski run or for a quick morning or afternoon outing.

Bill Williams Mountain

TERRAIN: **More Difficult**   TIME: **Full Day**
DISTANCE: **7 miles** one way
MAPS: **USGS—Bill Williams Mountain**
        USFS—South Kaibab

Bill Williams Mountain is composed of a cluster of volcanic domes and lava flows, dating from about four million years ago. Its double-peaked summit is home to telephone, radio, and television antennae and a fire lookout tower.

This is the western edge of northern Arizona's high country; views from the top of Bill Williams Mountain stretch across the Kaibab National Forest north to the Grand Canyon's North Rim, west to the Hualapai Mountains, south past Mingus Mountain to the Bradshaws, and east to the San Francisco Peaks. Spectacular views of the Sycamore Canyon/White Horse Lake area inspire ideas for ski tours along the rim of the Sycamore drainage.

South of Williams about four miles on FS 173 is a pullout for FS 111, the Bill Williams Lookout Road. Although the climb to the top of Bill Williams Mountain is gradual, the road gains over 1,500 feet in elevation and is regularly packed by a snow-cat checking the equipment on top of the mountain.

Near the upper saddle of the mountain, a turnoff leads to Chimney Rock Vista (Finger Rock on the forest service map). Chimney Rock is one of several volcanic remnants of lava conduits making up the Bill Williams volcanic field. Two miles farther up the lookout road are the final switchbacks to the summit—a good spot for a picnic, some pictures, and a rest before your well-earned descent back down the road.

Two alternatives exist on this tour. One is a climb via the Benham Trail, a hiking trail that begins just before the Lookout Road turnoff at the driveway to the Benham Ranch. Although this trail shortens the Lookout Road tour by one and a half to two miles, it may take longer and be much more work if it hasn't already been skiied in.

An alternative to the descent back down the lookout road is the snow course route on the northeast side of the mountain. This steep descent follows drainages to the old ski jump site (see Ski Jump Tour) and requires some knowledge of the mountain to prevent getting lost. This descent is rated Most Difficult; it is recommended for experienced backcountry skiers only.

To find the snow course descent, follow the road down from the summit and continue past the power lines on the east side of the mountain. In the middle of the straight stretch of the road past the power lines, look for red paint marks on the trees off the road. The descent follows the red paint marks down several hundred feet to the top of a steep gully. Continue down the gully until it meets a road. This is the road at the base of the old ski jump sight. From here, follow the road one mile to the parking area of the Williams Ski Run (see Ski Jump Tour). You will need a car shuttle back to the Bill Williams Lookout Road.

Ski Jump Tour/Bill Williams Mountain

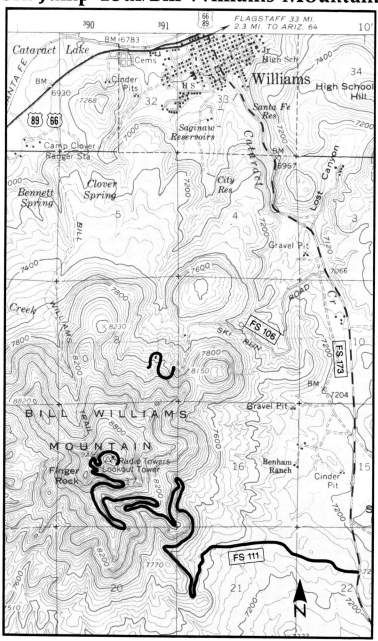

Government Prairie/Spring Valley

TERRAIN: **Easier to More Difficult** TIME: **Short to Full Day**
DISTANCE: **Variable**
MAPS: **USGS—Parks, Arizona**
USFS—Coconino, South Kaibab

Roughly fifteen miles west of Flagstaff, a vast cinder-cone-dotted prairie hides behind a front of ponderosa pines north of Interstate 40. This is Government Prairie, which holds two areas of interest for ski tourers: the Spring Valley Ski Trails and the Government Prairie cinder cones.

The Spring Valley Ski Trails, marked and maintained by the Kaibab National Forest, wind through the forest at the base of Sitgreaves Mountain. Their eastern exposure and layout help them hold snow well during the winter. One of the steeper trails climbs a gully to Eagle Rock viewpoint, a volcanic vent remnant that looks across the expanse of Government Prairie toward the San Francisco Peaks.

To get to the trails, drive north on Spring Valley Road (FS 141) from the Parks exit on I-40, seventeen miles from Flagstaff. The road passes private homes and some open areas before entering the trees and curving around to the Spring Valley Work Center and ski trailhead.

To the east of Spring Valley stretch the vast open fields of Government Prairie. From its southern end near the interstate, Government Prairie rolls for seven miles north to the foot of Kendrick Mountain. Several smooth-sided cinder cones lie around the edge of the prairie. Government Prairie has many possibilities for touring and with its open terrain, it is possible to choose your own route across the prairie and among the cinder cones. Some tourers come to ski the inviting cinder hills, while others enjoy skiing across the unrestricted flats, taking in views of the peaks high on the eastern skyline. From the parking area in Government Prairie, it is possible to ski across to the base of Kendrick Mountain and join up with FS 171 to FS 193, which leads to U.S. 180 near Deer Tanks.

Access to Government Prairie is best from the Parks exit on I-40. Head east from the Parks store on the service road FS 146 about a mile until turning north on FS 107. This road dead-ends at a parking area near Klostermeyer Hill. Though much of the prairie is on forest service land, there are many homes in the area whose privacy should be respected.

Government Prairie

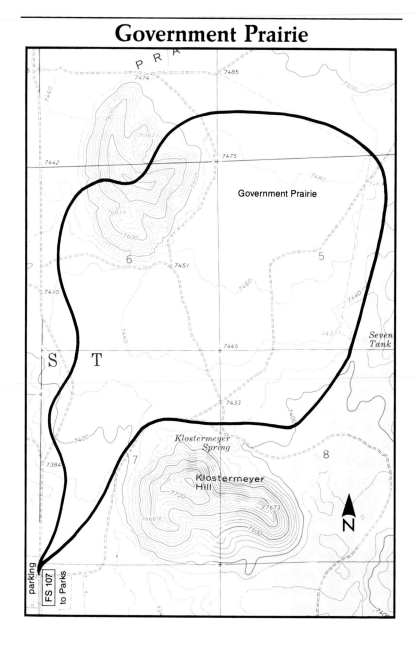

Spring Valley

GRAND CANYON NATIONAL PARK

Gliding along the rim country of the Grand Canyon on skis is a unique and rewarding way to experience its beauty and depth. While ski touring isn't commonly associated with the Grand Canyon, there are many miles of skiable terrain on the high forested rims of the canyon.

With a healthy snowfall, tours along the South Rim are possible along many of the dirt roads and trails that parallel or lead to the rim, such as the road to Shoshone Point or the Boundary Line Road west of Hermit's Rest. As elevation on the South Rim averages 6,500 feet, snow tends to melt soon after storms. For information on snow conditions along the rim, contact the Backcountry Office on the South Rim (see reference list page 133).

A thousand feet higher than its southern neighbor, the North Rim has reliable snow for most of the winter. At present the road into the North Rim closes during the winter. Although not in the immediate plans of the park, the North Rim may someday be kept open year round, altering the route of the North Rim Tour, but opening up other possibilities for tours along the rim from the lodge. Rangers living on the North Rim now groom part of the tour between there and Jacob Lake.

Ribbon Falls, a side stop of the North Rim Tour

North Rim Tour

TERRAIN: **More Difficult**   TIME: **Multiday**
DISTANCE: **65 miles**
MAPS: **USGS—Jacob Lake, De Motte Park, Bright Angel**
     USFS—North Kaibab (Note: Because this tour covers such a great
     distance, yet follows Arizona 67 from Jacob Lake to the North
     Rim, only the beginning portion of the tour is shown on the
     map herein. You will need to carry the maps indicated if plan-
     ning to complete the entire tour.)

Of the dozen tours into and around the North Rim, the most popular is the
classic route from Jacob Lake across the Kaibab Plateau to the North Rim and
on through the Grand Canyon, by foot, to the South Rim. In its nearly seventy-
mile length, the North Rim Tour covers over 10,000 feet of elevation change,
traverses four climatic zones, and transcends nearly 2.5 billion years of geologic
time.

The tour was first done in 1971 by Lee Dexter, an avid tourer and owner
of a local ski shop in Flagstaff. Over fifteen years later, the North Rim Tour remains uncrowded with usually less than twenty parties traversing the rim in a
winter. With the advent of skating techniques and lightweight ski equipment,
a long-sought challenge to complete the tour in one day was realized in 1986.
Starting at dawn on a side road twenty-five miles from the rim, Tim Coats, Lee
Dexter, and I ski-skated to the rim by noon and traversed the canyon to the South
Rim; total trip time was fifteen hours. The trip was later completed by another
party in twenty-two hours from Jacob Lake.

Despite these challenges, the tour is best enjoyed at a more leisurely pace.
Trips usually range from four to eight days, depending on conditions. Prior winter
camping experience is recommended for this tour, as temperatures along the
way can drop below zero and severe winter storms can move into the area suddenly and unexpectedly.

The elevated North Rim plateau (high point 9,200 feet) receives an average
of 150 inches of snow in the winter months; however, accumulations may be
as low as ninety inches or as high as 350 inches. The North Rim road from Jacob
Lake to the park, Arizona 67, is closed from mid-November through mid-May.
Skiing is often best from late February through April when spring conditions
make for faster skiing and little trail breaking.

The North Rim Tour begins at Jacob Lake, a small resort outpost at the junction of U.S. 89A and Arizona 67. There a locked gate closes the road to cars
and marks the start of the tour. During the first fifteen miles, Arizona 67 cuts
through the endless ponderosa pine forest of the Kaibab Plateau. At the base
of Telephone Hill, you enter Pleasant Valley, the first of a series of long open
valleys leading twenty-three miles to the park's entrance station. These valleys,
or parks, are a result of geologic faulting on the plateau and have no surface

drainage but drain through fissures in the underlying limestone. The longest of these valleys, De Motte Park, runs for eight miles and was named for Professor Harvey De Motte of Illinois, who worked on the plateau for the Powell survey in the summer of 1872.

A few miles past the entrance station to the national park, about thirty miles from Jacob Lake, Arizona 67 climbs to the top of Lindberg Hill before beginning an eight-mile, double-pole descent to the final hill that climbs to the rim at the head of the North Kaibab Trail. Here you are rewarded for the past days' labor by the solitude and winter scenery of the North Rim. The contrasts of color, cold, and snow are striking and give you plenty to marvel at before heading down the trail to Roaring Springs. If possible, try to schedule a layover day on the North Rim and tour out to one of several vista points along the rim, such as Uncle Jim, Bright Angel, or Widforss points.

With skis on your back, head down the winding North Kaibab Trail toward Roaring Springs. The trail usually loses its snow within a few miles; this is a good spot to change into some dry boots for the remainder of the tour. Along the upper reaches of the trail, ice flows often glaze the trail in some precarious spots. Instep crampons and a short rope can be useful when the trail looks hazardous. Check with park rangers for information on conditions and any special equipment that might be needed for your tour.

The fourteen-mile hike from the rim to the bottom of the canyon at Phantom Ranch follows the cool cascading waters of Bright Angel Creek below Roaring Springs. Allowing three days to traverse the canyon to the South Rim gives you plenty of time to stop and explore some of the side canyons on the way, such as Ribbon Falls or Phantom Creek. Standing at Phantom Ranch in a t-shirt and shorts is a satisfying juxtaposition to the cold snow country you just left on the rim.

There are two trails from Phantom Ranch to the South Rim, the Bright Angel and the South Kaibab. While the Kaibab is shorter but steeper (seven miles), the Bright Angel (eleven miles) has a campground and water along the way as well as facilities at the top.

Permits are required for any overnight trip into the national park. They can be obtained from the backcountry office on the South Rim. As mentioned above, special equipment, such as rope, ice axes, instep crampons, or snowshoes, is sometimes recommended for the trip, depending on snow and trail conditions. Also, preparing for the sun and the cold is important for the tour; plenty of sunscreen and a good visor will come in handy when reflection from the snow gets intense.

North Rim Tour

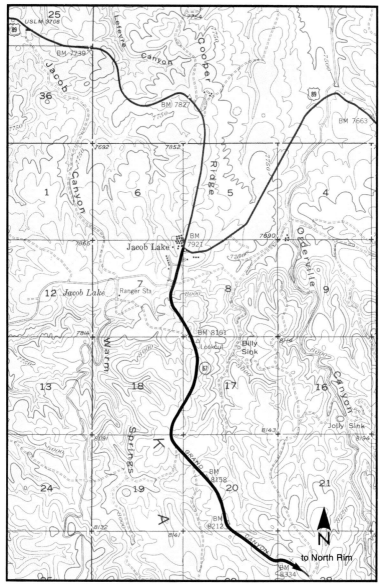

REGION 2

White Mountains

On the eastern margin of central Arizona, the long escarpment of the Mogollon Rim country is capped by a cluster of rounded, snow-capped peaks. These lofty summits make up the White Mountains, so named for the snow that lingers on their slopes for much of the year. Unlike their northern neighbors, the San Francisco Peaks, the White Mountains' descriptive name has held for centuries. To the local Apache Indian tribe, they are *Zil-clo-Ki-sa-on,* meaning "White Mountains," as does *Sierra Blanca,* the Spanish name for the range.

The thick aspen and mixed-conifer forest—Douglas fir, blue and Englemann spruce, and ponderosa pine—blankets all but the highest portions of the peaks; hence, Baldy Peak is an appropriate name for the range's highest summit (11,590 feet). The stand of ponderosa pine is the largest in the United States, extending from inside New Mexico, through the White Mountains and along the Mogollon Rim, up to the San Francisco Peaks.

Like much of the southern Colorado Plateau, the sedimentary strata of the White Mountains lies buried beneath thick layers of volcanic rock. Baldy Peak is at the center of a small cluster of stratovolcanoes that covered the region with lava two to ten million years ago. Later, over 200 cinder cones formed as lava sought new outlets to the surface when access through the central vents became blocked. During glacial times, the White Mountains were one of two areas in the state covered with and carved by caps of ice. The combination of volcanism and glacial erosion created the beautifully rounded topography that characterizes the White Mountains. This rolling terrain of meadows, valleys, and peaks often reminds one more of Rocky Mountain highlands than of desert plateaus.

The history of the White Mountains is like that of so many areas on the Colorado Plateau. Long the home of the White Mountain Apache Indian tribe, the region saw an influx of Spanish explorers beginning with Francisco Vasquez de Coronado in 1540. By the 1800s, Mormon families had moved into the area, expanding the range of the Mormon empire into the valley of the Little Colorado River. Range wars between settler and Indian, cattleman and sheepman, and outlaw and justice dominated the years to follow. In fact, Springerville was once thought to be the "worst town in the West" because of the number of rustlers, thieves, and gunslingers that found refuge in the vast, surrounding mountains. Later, railroads rolled into the forest of ponderosa pine, opening the White Mountains to the lumber industry.

Today, tourism plays a major role in White Mountain industry. Alpine skiers flock to the slopes of Sunrise Ski Area on the Apache Reservation, while ski tourers can take advantage of the excellent solitude and touring terrain near the towns of Greer and Alpine.

View from the windswept summit of Baldy Peak

GREER

Off the beaten path and tucked neatly alongside the West Fork of the Little Colorado River valley lies the town of Greer, Arizona. Formerly known as Lee Valley, the town of Greer gains its name from Americus Vespucius Greer, the first Mormon to settle the nearby Round Valley (now Springerville) in 1877.

In 1975 the Apache-Sitgreaves National Forest in cooperation with the town of Greer cut trails for cross-country skiers of all abilities just north of town. Although these trails are not described in this guidebook, they are well marked and easy to find. Just three miles south of Arizona 260 on the road to Greer (Arizona 373), a sign marks the pullout for the trail system. For information on snow conditions and trails, call the Chamber of Commerce or the Circle B Market in Greer (see reference list, page 133).

Pole Knoll

TERRAIN: **Easier**   TIME: **Half-day**
DISTANCE: **6 miles**
MAPS: **USGS—Greens Peak, Greer**
         USFS—Apache-Sitgreaves

As Arizona 260 climbs westward out of the Springerville valley and onto the plateau above, it passes into an open prairie surrounded by rounded cinder cones. To the south of the highway, as it enters the prairie, stands the tall, wooded cinder cone of Pole Knoll. Home of a fire lookout in the 1920s, Pole Knoll's aspen forest provided poles for use by local settlers. Although the cone is mostly forested now, a large and barren swath marks the western side of the hill, a favorite spot for telemarking when the snow is fresh.

The most popular Pole Knoll tour follows a trail around its base. The tour starts from the parking lot at the Pole Knoll Trailhead, on Arizona 260, just two miles west of the turnoff to Greer (Arizona 373). Blue trail markers lead along the north flank of the mountain and wind through thick groves of aspen and conifer, offering views north toward Greens Peak. The large aluminum fences that stretch across the open prairie below serve as breaks for the snow that often blows across the highway.

As it comes around the west side of Pole Knoll, the trail enters an opening at the base of the large swath that climbs to the knoll's top. When conditions are right, this is a good spot to practice carving some telemark turns. Views west from here show the ski slopes of Sunrise Ski Area, with Baldy Peak far to the south. Continuing along the trail to the south, skiers can connect with the ski trail system leading to Greer, four miles away.

To return to the Pole Knoll Trailhead, follow the trail up a moderately steep ravine, then down a long, gentle hill toward the parking area.

Pole Knoll

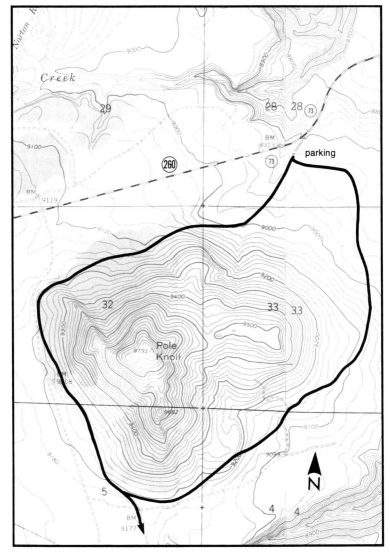

Fish Creek

TERRAIN: **Easier**   TIME: **Short Day**
DISTANCE: **2 miles**
MAPS: **USGS—Greens Peak**
      USFS—Apache-Sitgreaves

Perhaps one of the most popular and accessible touring spots in the Lee Valley area is Fish Creek. Draining the prairie west of Pole Knoll, Fish Creek parallels Arizona 260 until it drops off the high plateau to the east.

Just over a mile east of the Pole Knoll Trailhead, parking is available at FS 113F on the south side of the highway. This road heads around the west side of Pole Knoll toward White Mountain Reservoir. To get to Fish Creek, cross Arizona 260 to the north and ski through the small grove of aspen trees just off the road. Continuing through the grove leads to the small valley of the creek. From here, it is possible to tour up and down the valley of Fish Creek at your leisure (watch for water in the creek bottom!). The slopes of the valley often hold snow late in the season and provide good areas for practicing hill techniques. Return via the same route.

Valley of the Little Colorado River

Fish Creek

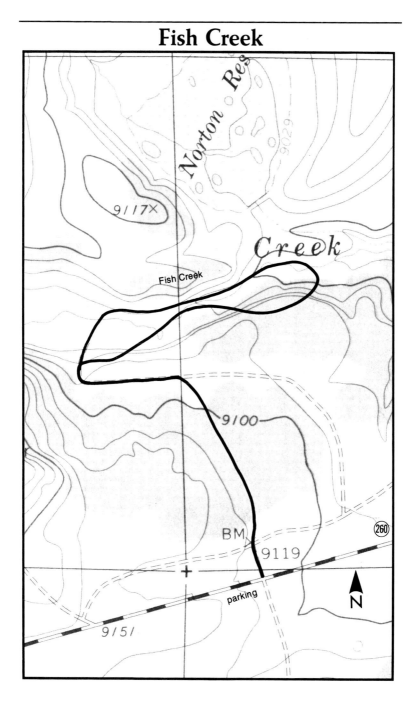

Greens Peak

TERRAIN: **More Difficult** TIME: **Full Day**
DISTANCE: **6 miles** one way
MAPS: **USGS—Greens Peak**
  USFS—Apache-Sitgreaves

Like many of the prominent summits in this area, Greens Peak was given its name by Captain George M. Wheeler in 1873 to honor Calvary officer Colonel John Green, then stationed at Camp Apache. Presently the home of a fire lookout and several radio towers, the summit of this large cinder cone offers superb views of the White Mountains and surrounding area.

The trip to Greens Peak is popular for many ski tourers, as it is easily accessible and, except for the final climb, follows mostly gentle terrain. However, this also makes it a popular trip for snowmobilers, and it is not unusual for the road to be busy with activity most winter weekends.

Three miles east of the Sunrise Ski Area turnoff (Arizona 273), or five miles west of the Greer road (Arizona 373), FS 117 joins Arizona 260. Park here and ski the road north along the edges of several large meadows for five miles to a junction. Take the left fork, FS 61, until it joins FS 61C, which climbs the final distance up to the Greens Peak summit (10,134 feet). Returning down the road can be exciting, but caution is needed. With adequate snow, it is possible to ski down the long slopes off the road of Greens Peak back to FS 61. From there, follow FS 117 back to the highway.

Greens Peak

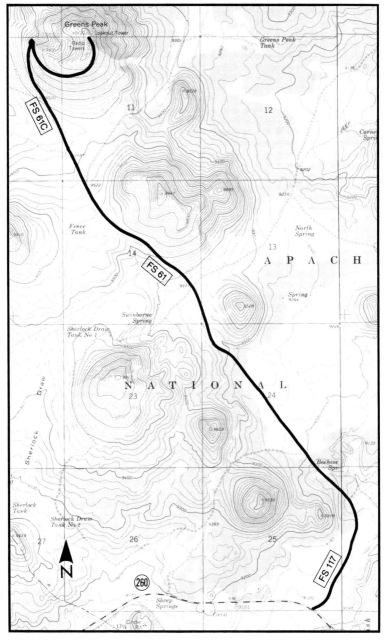

Sheep Crossing

TERRAIN: **Easier**   Time: **Full Day**
DISTANCE: **4 miles** one way
MAPS: **USGS—Mount Ord (Mount Baldy** on new editions)
      USFS—Apache-Sitgreaves

A major route of commerce and confrontation once passed through the serene West Fork of the Little Colorado River, high in the White Mountains near Greer. This was the trail along which flocks of sheep massed each year on their annual migration up and down from their high summer pastures to the packing houses in Phoenix. Sheep Crossing served as one of the many important crossings along that route and was the site of several violent disputes that arose between sheepmen and cattlemen competing for grazing rights in the rich highlands of the White Mountains. Today, Sheep Crossing marks the eastern boundary and access point to the Mt. Baldy Wilderness Area, created in 1970.

The tour into Sheep Crossing follows the edge of a vast cinder-cone-studded meadow for four miles before joining the Little Colorado River's West Fork. While the river valley is well worth the tour, there is plenty of good touring on the large meadow above. Several short tours along the forest's edge or forays across the meadow are also worth exploring.

From Arizona 260, turn south on Arizona 273 toward Sunrise Ski Area. Two miles past the ski area driveway, Arizona 273 turns into FS 113 at the gate that marks its closure for the winter at the forest service boundary. In most snow years it is possible to start skiing here. However, when the snow is low, it is possible to drive around the gate to the right and continue farther on FS 113. When snow is low enough to drive all the way to Sheep Crossing, ski in the Mount Baldy Wilderness Area (see Mount Baldy Wilderness).

From the gate, FS 113 passes through open meadows and along the west margin of White Mountain Reservoir, a popular migratory stop for waterfowl and birds of prey. Within two miles, FS 87 to Greer joins the road. Just past here and over a small hill, FS 113 enters the valley of the West Fork of the Little Colorado River.

Originating from springs on the flanks of Baldy Peak, the West Fork passes through a once-glaciated valley and onto its confluence with the East Fork near Greer. Within a mile, FS 113 crosses the river and climbs out of the valley, leading to Lee Valley Reservoir in another two and a half miles. By not crossing the river and continuing along its north side for one mile, you will reach Sheep Crossing. Return via the same route.

Just before Sheep Crossing there is evidence of an abandoned railroad bed, part of the Apache Railway, a narrow-gauge train that once ran lumber from a logging operation in Maverick to the sawmill in McNary, sixty-eight miles away. Built in 1949, the train's load eventually changed from timber to tourists, until its final dismantling in the sixties.

Mount Baldy Wilderness

TERRAIN: **Most Difficult**   TIME: **Full Day or Multiday**
DISTANCE: **7 miles** one way from Sheep Crossing
MAPS: **USGS—Mount Ord (Mount Baldy)**
       USFS—Apache-Sitgreaves

The tour to Mount Baldy (11,590 feet) is one of the most scenic, spectacular, and demanding tours in the White Mountains. Although most of the tour lies on forest service land, the last quarter-mile to Baldy's summit is on the Apache Indian Reservation. Permission from the tribe is required for entering the reservation. (For further information, contact the Fort Apache Tribal Office in White River. See reference list, page 133.)

Access to the wilderness area varies depending on snow conditions. When the snow level is low, it is possible to drive the four miles to Sheep Crossing (see Sheep Crossing Tour); when snow is abundant, it is necessary to ski in from the gate on FS 113, making the round-trip tour to Baldy a total of twenty-two miles. In the latter case, it is often best to ski in and snow camp near Sheep Crossing. From there it is possible to ski to Mount Baldy as a day trip.

From Sheep Crossing, the Mount Baldy trail heads upriver along the West Fork of the Little Colorado River. The grade is gentle and the scenery tremendous. A long series of open meadows follows the creek upward, offering glimpses of Mount Baldy on the western skyline with the broad summit of Mount Thomas before it. Although the name appears on the forest service map, Mount Thomas is not marked on the Mount Ord topographic map.

Two miles from Sheep Crossing, the trail enters the trees at the head of a large open meadow. Particular attention to the trail must be paid here, as trail markers are infrequent and the trail is vague. The many meanders of the creek, coming from springs above, create deep gullies that can be treacherous on skis. The trail eventually works its way onto the saddle between Mount Baldy and Mount Thomas. From here, views of the Lee Valley area are unobstructed in almost every direction.

This pass is a major division point in the drainage of the lower Colorado River. On the north side, snowmelt forms the headwaters of the Little Colorado River, which drains north and west to meet the Colorado River in the bottom of the Grand Canyon. To the south, water runs southwest through the drainages of the Black, Salt, and Gila rivers, eventually meeting the Colorado River near Yuma, almost a thousand miles downstream from the Little Colorado River's confluence with the Colorado.

From here, the final climb to Mount Baldy's summit lies on the Apache Indian Reservation. Permits are required beyond this point. Several switchbacks lead up to the peak's broad summit ridge. As unlikely as it may seem, on the steep east faces of the ridge are the scars of avalanches, which may pose a threat during unstable conditions.

Sheep Crossing/Mt. Baldy Wilderness

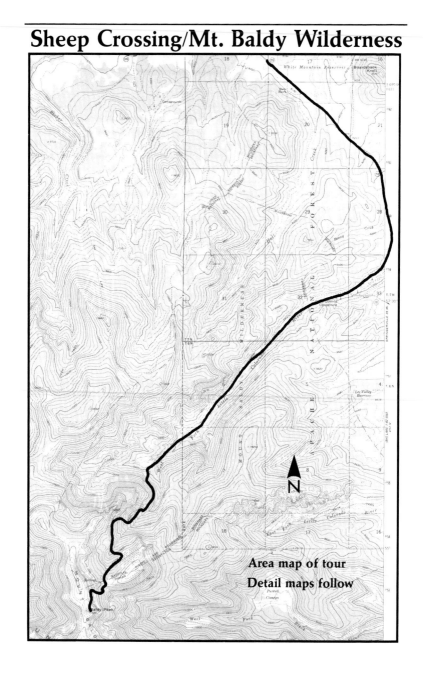

Area map of tour

Detail maps follow

Sheep Crossing/Mt. Baldy Wilderness

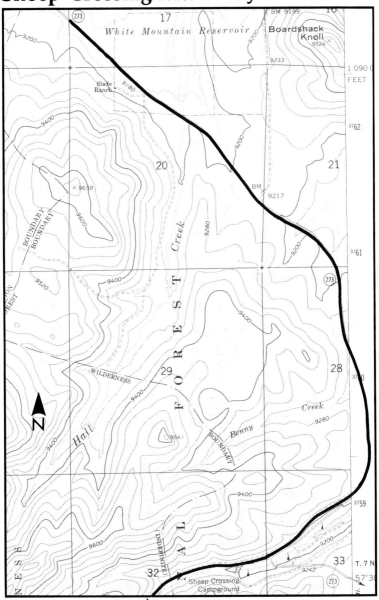

MAP 1 OF 3

Sheep Crossing/Mt. Baldy Wilderness

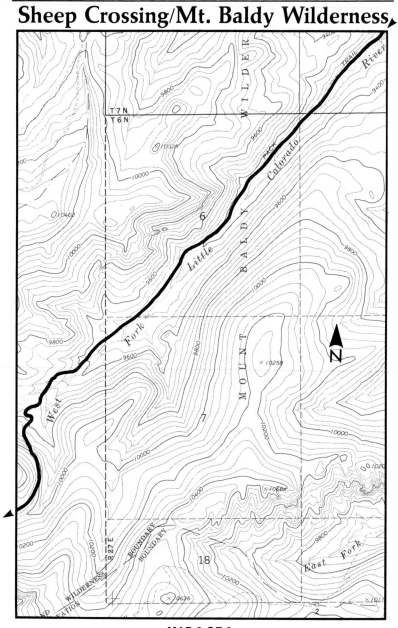

MAP 2 OF 3

Sheep Crossing/Mt. Baldy Wilderness

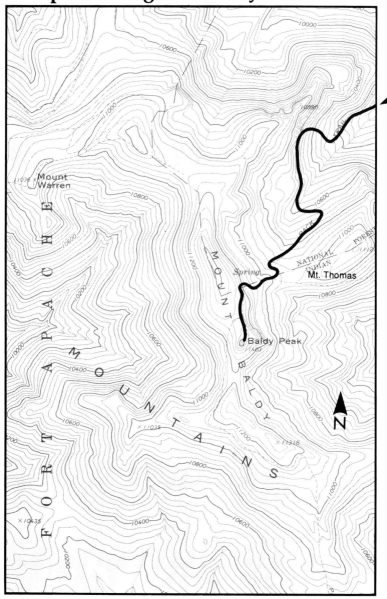

MAP 3 OF 3

ALPINE

Nestled high in a mountain valley south of Springerville along U.S. 666, is the small town of Alpine. Its 8,000-foot elevation and proximity to the conifer forests and mountainous terrain of the White Mountains make it a refreshing and reliable spot for ski touring.

Formerly known as Bush Valley, home of Fort Bush, the area was later called Frisco for the San Francisco River that meanders through the valley and irrigates some of the most elevated arable land in the nation. As Mormon settlers from Alpine, Utah, moved into the area in the mid-1800s, they brought with them the name of their former home and gave it to their new one because of its picturesque and mountainous setting. One of these early settlers, Fred Hamblin, was probably related to the famous Mormon pioneer and explorer Jacob Hamblin, who died in 1886 and was buried in Alpine.

The Alpine area offers good access to a number of forest service roads in the surrounding national forest. As in the Greer area, there are several ski trails marked by the Apache National Forest. Information on forest trails and snow conditions can be obtained from the ranger station in Alpine (see reference list, page 133).

Williams Valley

TERRAIN: **Easier**   TIME: **Short Day**
DISTANCE: **1 to 5 miles**
MAPS: **USGS—Alpine, Arizona**
        USFS—Apache-Sitgreaves

The Williams Valley area offers some of the closest and most accessible touring terrain to the town of Alpine. For many years it has been the training spot for the cross-country ski team of Alpine.

Just two and a half miles north of Alpine on U.S. 666, FS 249 turns west and follows a plowed road three miles to the edge of Williams Valley. It is possible to park along the road in several places and ski up and down the length of the valley. Several roads leave the valley to the south and climb to hidden meadows in the forest that are worth exploring.

Williams Valley

Escudilla Mountain / Terry Flat

TERRAIN: **More Difficult**   TIME: **Full Day or Multiday**
DISTANCE: **5 miles** one way
MAPS: **USGS—Alpine, Arizona**
     USFS—Apache-Sitgreaves

On the edge of the White Mountains, near the New Mexico border, a dark and impressive flat-topped mountain dominates the highland horizon for miles around. This is Escudilla, or "dark blue pot," Mountain (10,912 feet). Beneath its long rim and hidden from view, the protected valley of Terry Flat (9,500 feet) lies covered with snow for longer than most touring spots in the Alpine area. A rich forest, largely of aspen, covers the hills around Terry Flat, replacing a thick conifer forest destroyed by fire in 1951.

In contrast to its present commanding height, the summit of Escudilla Mountain once lay at the bottom of a large ravine. During previous volcanic episodes, the ravine served as a channel for flowing lavas. With time and weathering, the softer sediments of the ravine's bordering ridges eroded away, leaving its lava-capped bottom a lofty plateau. Further weathering carved the convoluted topography of Escudilla Mountain.

Near the divide between Nutrioso and Alpine along U.S. 666, FS 56 climbs east into Escudilla Mountain past Hulsey Lake to Terry Flat. As with many forest roads, snow conditions determine how far in it is possible to drive. Often it is good to park by a barricaded logging road one mile past the Hulsey Lake turn-off. The road up to Terry Flat is often patchy with drifted snow in spots. A combined ski and walk up the five-mile road will take you across a steep-sided road-cut and onto a forked junction. These forks begin the six-mile loop that encircles the forests and meadows of Terry Flat. The right fork leads about a mile to Terry Flat, and the left fork crosses Tool Box Draw and the Escudilla Lookout Trailhead within a half-mile and leads to Terry Flat within another mile.

In the late 1970s, the ski club in Alpine built a small cabin on the northern edge of Terry Flat. It is located in the first open area a half-mile south of Tool Box Draw and just to the west of the Terry Flat road. (For information on cabin use, contact the forest service ranger station in Alpine.) This cabin provides a good spot for picnicking, or even a base camp for skiers wanting to spend a weekend doing day trips or moonlight skiing on the mountain.

To the west of Terry Flat, abandoned logging roads lead through the woods toward several clearings on Escudilla's rim. From here it is possible to look down toward the road to Alpine and across to the Baldy Peak area. Another excellent tour heads up the Escudilla Lookout Trail, which begins just south of where the Terry Flat road (FS 56) crosses Tool Box Draw. The three-mile trip up to the lookout tower passes across some spectacular open hillside country and allows an excellent overview of Escudilla Mountain in its entirety. In low snow years, it may be possible to drive all the way into the trailhead itself.

Escudilla Mountain/Terry Flat

Peeling bark, White Mountains

HANNAGAN MEADOW*

Moving from New Mexico in the 1890s, Robert Hannagan ran cattle in a high mountain pasture in the White Mountains. However, Hannagan left the area soon after being chained to a tree by two men interested in collecting the $1,200 he owed them. That was the only summer Hannagan spent with his cattle in the meadows that now bear his name.

At 9,000 feet elevation, the Hannagan Meadow area has some of the earliest and latest snow in the White Mountains. Although this area is popular for snowmobilers, there are ski-touring trails maintained by the forest service and Hannagan Meadow Lodge that run through the national forest and into the Blue Range Primitive Area that are off limits to snowmobiling. Information on snow conditions can be obtained by calling Hannagan Meadow Lodge or the ranger station in Alpine. Hannagan Meadow can be reached by following U.S. 666 south of Alpine for twenty-two miles. For information on snow conditions, call Hannagan Meadow Lodge (see reference list, page 133).

Carving telemark turns in spring snow, White Mountains

---

*There exists a difference of opinion regarding the correct spelling of Hannagan. We use this spelling because the nature of this book requires coincidence with actual maps and road signs. This does not, however, imply that ours is the correct spelling.

Clell Lee Trail

TERRAIN: **Easier**   TIME: **Half-day**
DISTANCE: **4 miles**
MAPS: **USGS—Hannagan Meadow**
    USFS—Apache-Sitgreaves

Clell Lee was once a prominent figure in the valley of the Blue River. A rancher and hunting guide, Clell would move up and down seasonally between his Blue River and Hannagan Meadow homes. Known worldwide for the lion hunting dogs he raised, Clell traveled to Africa on several occasions, as well as many other countries, for his expertise as a lion-hunting guide. Clell died in the mid-1970s, and the trail that passes by his summer cabin near Hannagan Meadow carries his name.

Across the meadow from the Hannagan Meadow Lodge parking area, a ski trail marked by orange trail markers climbs into the woods and follows a gentle, descending valley past the old Lee Cabin. Nearby are the kennels that once housed his prized lion-hunting dogs. Farther down the valley, the trail turns, rejoins the highway, and begins the climb back up to the meadow.

KP Rim / Willow Spring Trail

TERRAIN: **More Difficult**   TIME: **Half-day**
DISTANCE: **6 miles**
MAPS: **USGS—Hannagan Meadow**
    USFS—Apache-Sitgreaves

This tour enters the Blue River Primitive Area and is closed to snowmobile use. Across from the Hannagan Meadow Lodge, orange trail markers lead a hundred yards to a fork. The left fork is the Clell Lee Trail (see previous tour), and the right fork heads south and west into the woods. Within a mile, the trail passes through the Hannagan Forest Service Camp and descends into the head of Grant Creek. After some steep sections in the drainage, the trail climbs out and passes in and out of open meadows in the forest. At this point, the trail follows the Steeple Creek Trail and begins a long loop back toward the highway. In this section, there are several scenic views into the KP drainage and beyond. At U.S. 666, it is possible to follow the road for three miles back to the Hannagan Meadow Lodge. Many skiers prefer to avoid the return ski along the highway by doing a car shuttle.

Clell Lee/KP Rim/Willow Spring Trail

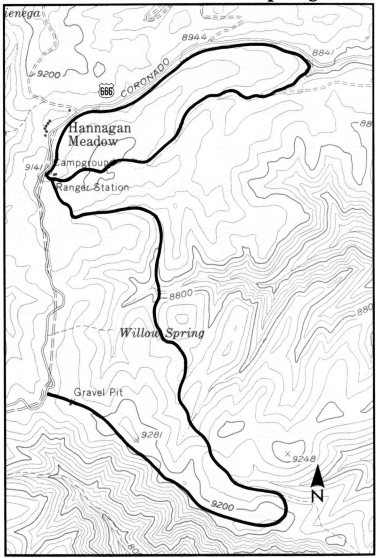

Reno Lookout Road/Corduroy Creek

TERRAIN: **Easier**   TIME: **Short Day**
DISTANCE: **2 miles**
MAPS:**USGS—Hannagan Meadow**
    USFS—Apache-Sitgreaves

As U.S. 666 climbs toward the Mogollon Rim south of Hannagan Meadow Lodge, the snow improves and there are several open clearcuts easily reached from the road. Their flat valley bottoms and hilly sides make these fun play spots for a quick tour.

The road to Reno Lookout, FS 25, turns west from the highway just before reaching the rim. Park here and instead of following FS 25, ski down an abandoned road that leads to the right and takes you to the first of a series of clearcuts that line the head of Corduroy Creek.

Forest Service 25 continues on toward Reno Lookout and provides some pleasurable touring across rolling terrain, although the area can be heavily used by snowmobiles at times. The tour to Reno Lookout is seven miles one way and takes a long day to ski in and out.

Upper drainage of the Little Colorado River, Mount Baldy in the distance

Reno Lookout Road/Corduroy Creek

REGION 3

Mogollon Rim

The southern boundary of the Colorado Plateau ends abruptly in Arizona along the rugged escarpment of the Mogollon Rim. It is across this craggy region that the high plateau of the Four Corners region ends and the conifer forests drop quickly to meet the pinyon and sage country of the desert below. During the winter, blankets of snow cover the ground, opening many roads for touring that offer an experience unique to Arizona: gliding silently through the conifer forests while viewing the desert below.

With good elevation (8,000 feet) and majestic views, the Mogollon Rim country has all the makings for excellent touring. Many miles of forest service roads wind along the plateau out to vista points or along the rim itself.

Sheep Spring Point

TERRAIN: **Easier**   TIME: **Half-day**
DISTANCE: **3 miles** one way
MAPS: **USGS—Woods Canyon, Arizona USFS—Apache-Sitgreaves**

Several popular short to half-day tours begin on Arizona 260 at Forest Lakes and head south on forest service roads to scenic viewpoints at the rim. The tour to Sheep Spring Point follows an unnumbered dirt road for three rolling miles to the rim, where it overlooks OW Ranch and the Canyon Creek Fish Hatchery. With extended sunny periods, several exposed parts of the trail tend to burn off quickly, so this is a good tour to catch soon after a storm.

North Point

TERRAIN: **Easier**   TIME: **Half-day**
DISTANCE: **4 miles**
MAPS: **USGS—Woods Canyon, Arizona USFS—Apache-Sitgreaves**

More reliable snow can be found on the two-mile tour to North Point, which begins at the Canyon Point Campground (FS 238) and rolls through the forest to the rim west of Sheep Spring Point.

Sheep Spring Point/North Point

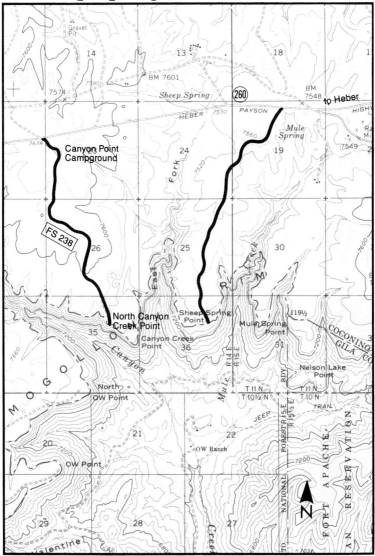

Woods Canyon Lake

TERRAIN: **Easier**   TIME: **Half-day**
DISTANCE: **4 miles** one way
MAPS: **USGS—Woods Canyon, Arizona**
      USFS—Apache-Sitgreaves

West of Forest Lakes, several good tours wind along parts of the General Crook Trail toward Promontory Butte. Near where Arizona 260 crosses the rim, FS 300 leads north and west into the forest. This road is usually plowed for parking. Around two and a half miles up FS 300, the road branches. Here, follow the north fork, FS 150, for a pleasant day tour to Woods Canyon Lake. Return via the same route.

Promontory Lookout / Butte

TERRAIN: **More Difficult**   TIME: **Full or Multiday**
DISTANCE: **10 miles**
MAPS: **USGS—Woods Canyon, Promontory Butte**
      USFS—Apache-Sitgreaves

Follow the same route described in the Woods Canyon tour (previous) until FS 300 branches. Continue on FS 300 to Promontory Lookout Tower, where views over the rim are tremendous. From a camp near the lookout, an excellent day trip can be skied along FS 76 to the end of Promontory Butte, a peninsula extending south from the rim.

The multiday tour can be skied from Arizona 260 to U.S. 87, or the other way around. Choosing the former, you will ski beyond Promontory Butte and meander in and out from the rim until finally reaching Baker Butte in the Coconino National Forest. Although this route is skied from time to time, snow conditions vary greatly depending on the season and storms. The best local source of information on the snow conditions may be from the Forest Lakes Touring Center in Forest Lakes.

Woods Canyon/Promontory Lookout

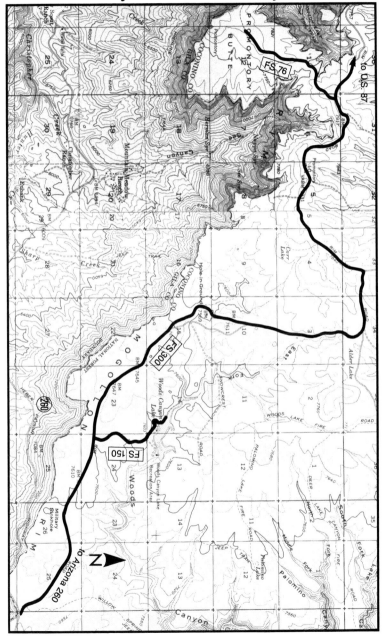

Swift Trail, Mount Graham

REGION 4

Southern Arizona

In the southeastern corner of Arizona, three snowcapped ranges dot the route from Tucson to the New Mexico border. As unlikely as it seems, the Santa Catalinas, Mount Graham, and the Chiricahua Mountains hold incredible possibilities for the southern Arizona ski tourer, all within a day's drive of Tucson. The unique and unbelievable juxtaposition of ski touring through cool, evergreen forests while enjoying the views of vast desertscapes below is something worth experiencing.

Although snow conditions in these ranges fluctuate from year to year, there are usually several times each season when snowfall is sufficient for good ski touring. For information regarding skiing conditions in southern Arizona, contact the Summit Hut in Tucson (see reference list, page 133).

Santa Catalinas / Mount Lemmon

TERRAIN: **Easier to More Difficult** TIME: **Short Day to Half-day**
DISTANCE: **Variable**
MAPS: **USGS—Mount Lemmon, Bellota Ranch**
         USFS—Coronado (Safford and Santa Catalina Ranger Districts)

Dominating the skyline north of Tucson, the Santa Catalinas rise to an elevation of 9,157 feet. The elevation, exposure, and easy access up the twenty-five-mile Santa Catalina Highway from Tucson make the Mount Lemmon area popular for tours in the snowy season.

There are a number of ski-touring areas off the Mount Lemmon Road. The tour down Rose Canyon is off limits to four wheelers and offers quiet skiing toward Rose Canyon Lake. Due to its elevation, Rose Canyon is best skied after a good, cold storm.

Farther up the road, tours in the Organization Ridge/Palisade Ranger Station area are popular and offer some of the only limited, plowed parking on the mountain. Touring through the Soldier Camp Summer Home Area toward Soldiers Lake, south of the highway, is pleasant after a storm. The tour to Mount Bigelow and Bear Wallow follows a north-facing road that holds snow well. The highest touring spot on the mountain is the ridge road to Lemmon Rock Lookout; access is often possible past the Summerhaven Ski Area lodge.

Santa Catalinas/Mt. Lemmon

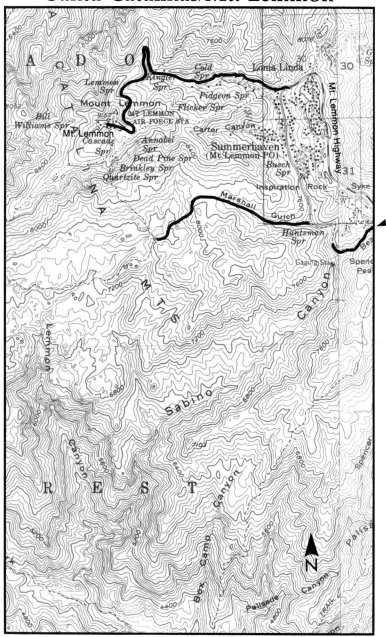

MAP 2 OF 2

Santa Catalinas/Mt. Lemmon

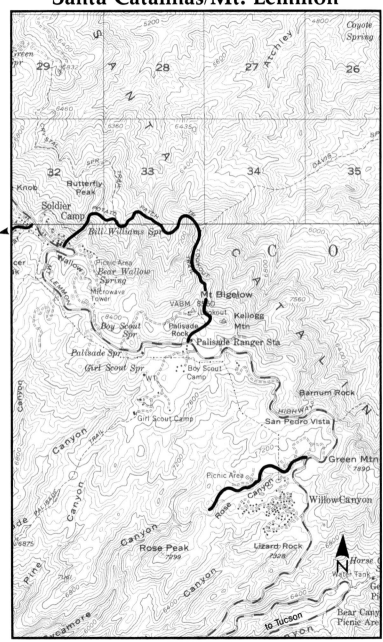

MAP 1 OF 2

Buena Vista Peak, Chiricahua Mountains

Chiricahua Mountains

TERRAIN: **Easier to More Difficult** TIME: **Half-day to Multiday**
DISTANCE: **Variable**
MAPS:**USGS—Cochise Head, Chiricahua Peak, Portal**
    USFS—Coronado (Chiricahua, Peloncillo, Dragoon
    Mountain Ranges)

The Chiricahua Mountains' array of strikingly eroded outcrops is as rugged as the Apache people for whom they are named. These were the people who proudly resisted U.S. domination for many years, fighting under such legendary leaders as Cochise and Geronimo. In 1924 the beauty and character of the range was protected by the establishment of the Chiricahua National Monument.

Despite their ruggedness, the high ridge that forms the crest of the range has good terrain for ski touring. To reach the Chiricahuas, drive south from I-10 at Wilcox on Arizona 186 to the Chiricahua National Monument turnoff. This is the Pinery Canyon road that leads to Onion Saddle and over the range to Portal, Arizona. Drive up the road as far as snow conditions allow, then ski to Onion Saddle. From here, a winding road branches south toward Buena Vista Peak (8,823 feet) and Rustler's Park, both popular destinations. Longer multiday treks across the range are possible for the adventurous ski tourer.

Chiricahua Mountains

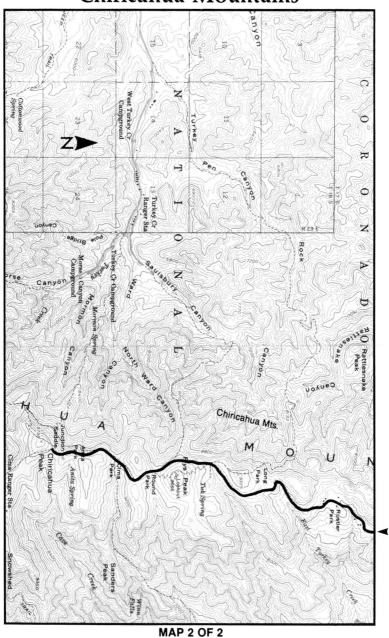

MAP 2 OF 2

Chiricahua Mountains

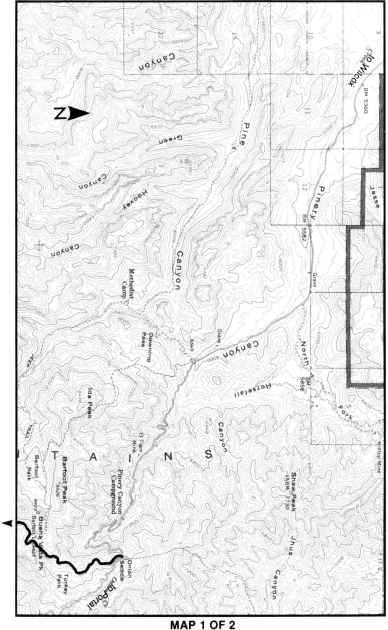

MAP 1 OF 2

Mount Graham / Pinaleno Mountains

TERRAIN: **Easier to More Difficult** TIME: **Half-day to Multiday**
DISTANCE: **Variable**
MAPS:**USGS—Mount Graham, Webb Peak, Stockton Pass**
       USFS—Coronado (Safford and Santa Catalina Ranger Districts)

Formerly known as Sierra Bonita, the Pinaleno Mountains rise dramatically from the Sulphur Springs Valley, south of Safford. The range is commonly called Mount Graham, or the Grahams, the name of the summit peak. Which Graham was eternalized here in the 1800s remains a matter of conjecture, as there were several prominent Grahams during this period.

With perhaps the best and most reliable snow conditions of the southern Arizona ranges, Mount Graham offers many miles of excellent rolling terrain for skiing. The main road up the mountain from Safford (Arizona 366) is usually drivable to near Turkey Flat, which is nice for touring. Beyond here, it is possible to catch a ride or ski toward the mountain's higher elevations. Once on top, a long ridge road links several areas of skiable terrain worth exploring. Numerous roads can be skied in the areas of Hospital Flat, Grant Hill, and Soldier Creek.

Another road leads to Mount Graham's summit (10,720 feet), where you get a tremendous view of the Sulphur Springs Valley down the eastern escarpment of the mountain. At the end of the ridge road lies Riggs Lake, offering good skiing and scenery as does the area near the town of Old Columbine. Tours to farther reaches of the mountain may require a multiday effort. From a central camp on the mountain, access to several of these areas would be possible as day tours.

Mount Graham/Pinaleno Mountains

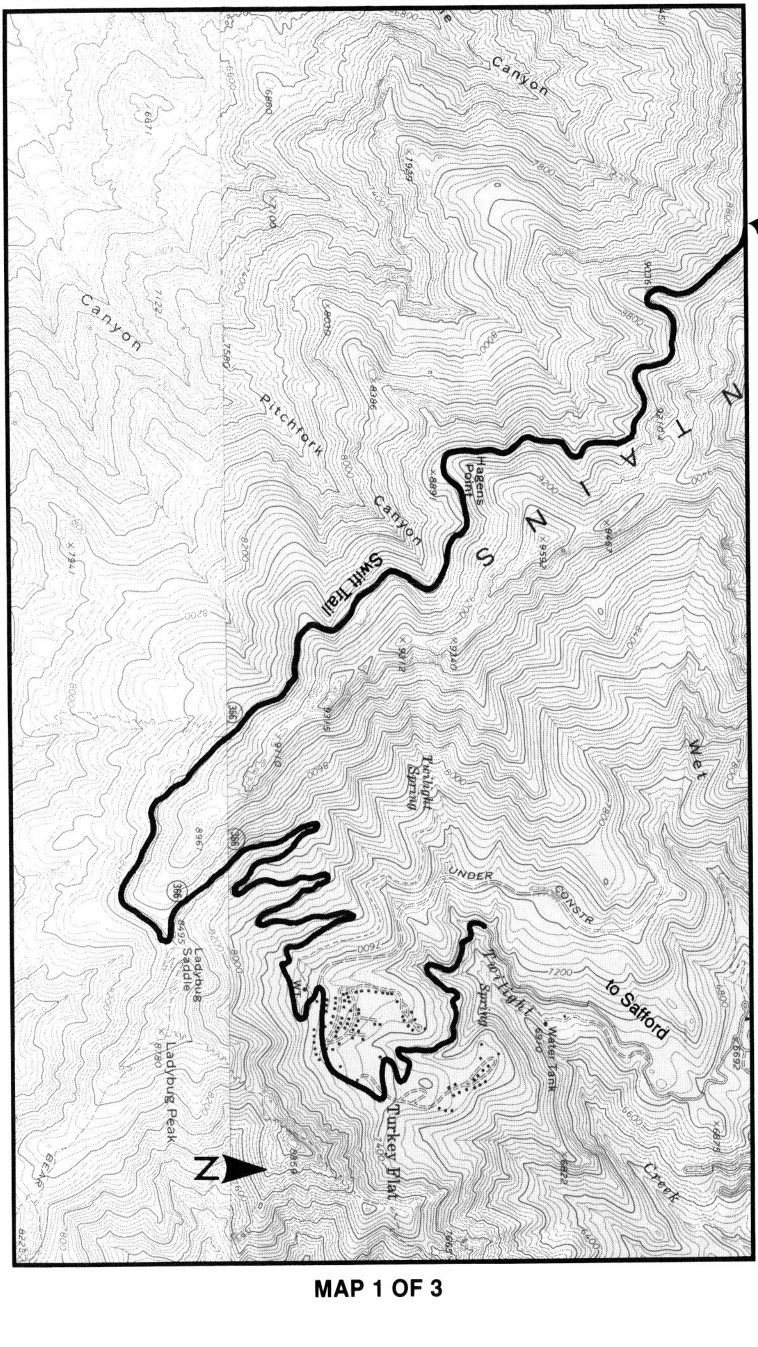

MAP 1 OF 3

Mount Graham/Pinaleno Mountains

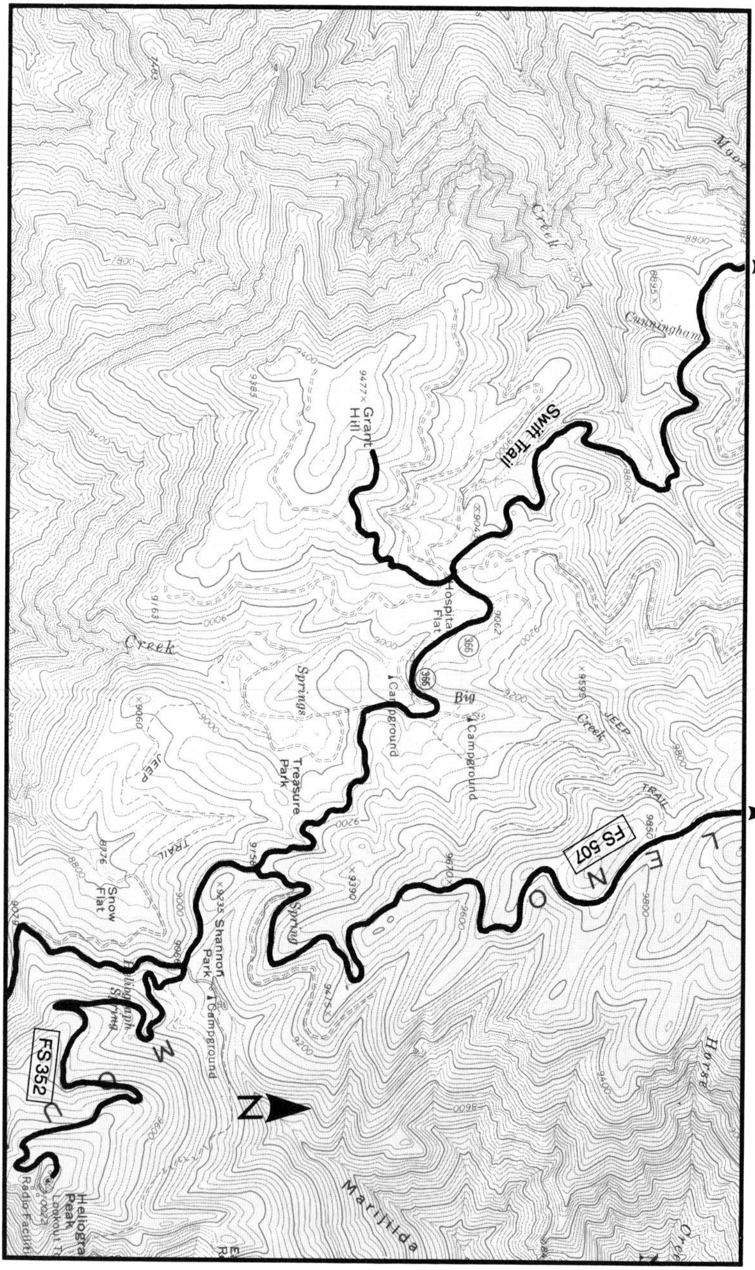

MAP 2 OF 3

Mount Graham/Pinaleno Mountains

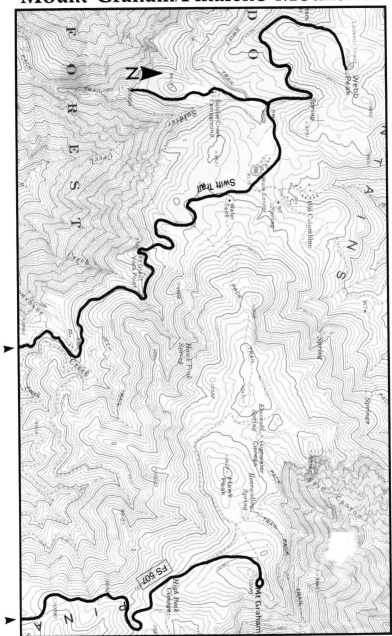

MAP 3 OF 3

In Closing . . .

Although the tours in this book provide a broad choice of country to explore, they by no means exhaust ski-touring possibilities in Arizona. By using this book, skiers will hopefully find variations, combinations, or even whole new tours to ski.

Because snow levels fluctuate greatly in Arizona, there are other areas not mentioned in this book that are skiable from time to time. Such places include the Bradshaw Mountains south of Prescott, the Hualapai Mountains near Kingman, the rim country above Sedona and Payson, and along both the north and south rims of the Grand Canyon.

Use this guide as a reference. Take it with you, make notes about what you find, and enjoy the unique snow and backcountry of Arizona's snowy plateaus. I'd be interested in hearing your comments on this guidebook as well as any new information on tours and areas you've explored. Please contact me through my publisher.

Heading home from ski tour, San Francisco Peaks

WHO TO CONTACT

The following reference list may be useful for planning a ski outing. The government agencies listed below are valuable for providing information on permits, snow conditions, or road conditions. For more specific information on snow, waxing, trails, maps, equipment, and such, contact one of the local specialty ski shops or touring centers.

Northern Arizona
Arizona Department of Public Safety
Road Conditions, Northern Arizona
779-2711

Coconino National Forest
2519 E. Seventh Ave.
Flagstaff, AZ 86001
527-7470

Flagstaff Nordic Center
Route 4, Box 958
Flagstaff, AZ 86001
774-6216

Grand Canyon National Park
Backcountry Office
Box 129
Grand Canyon, AZ 86023
638-2474
North Rim Ranger 638-2622

Kaibab National Forest
Chandler Ranger District
501 W. Bill Williams Dr.
Williams, AZ 86046
635-2676

Mormon Lake and Montezuma Ski Trails
Mormon Lake Lodge
Box 12
Mormon Lake, AZ 86038
774-0462

White Mountains
Apache-Sitgreaves National Forest
Alpine Ranger District
Alpine, AZ 85920
339-4384

Greer Ranger District
Greer, AZ 85927
735-7558

Forest Lakes Touring Center
Box 1887
Heber, AZ 85931
535-4047

Greer Ski Trails
Circle B Market
Box 121
Greer, AZ 85927
735-7540

Hannagan Meadow Lodge
Box 335
Alpine, AZ 85920
339-4370

White Mountain Apache Tribe
Box 700
White River, AZ 85941
338-4346

Southern Arizona
Chiricahua National Monument
Dos Cabezas Star Route
Wilcox, AZ 85643
824-3460

Coronado National Forest
Safford Ranger District
504 5th Ave.
Safford, AZ 85546
428-4150

Summit Hut
4044 E. Speedway
Tucson, AZ 85712
325-1554

Index to Tours

| White Horse Hills | More Difficult | 5 miles[2] | Full Day | 48 |
| Wing Mountain* | More Difficult | 7.5 miles | Half-day | 38 |

REGION 2: WHITE MOUNTAINS

Clell Lee Trail*	Easier	4 miles	Half-day	112
Escudilla Mountain*	More Dificult	8 miles[2]	Full or Multi-day	108
Fish Creek	Easier	2 miles	Short Day	96
Greens Peak	More Difficult	6 miles[2]	Full Day	98
KP Rim/Willow Spring	More Difficult	6 miles	Half-day	112
Mount Baldy*	Most Difficult	7 miles[3]	Full or Multiday	101
Pole Knoll	Easier	6 miles	Half-day	94
Reno Lookout/ Corduroy Creek	Easier	2 miles	Short Day	114
Sheep Crossing	Easier	4 miles[2]	Full Day	100
Terry Flat*	More Difficult	5 miles[2]	Full Day	108
Williams Valley*	Easier	1 to 5 miles	Short Day	106

REGION 3: MOGOLLON RIM

North Point	Easier	4 miles	Half-day	116
Promontory Lookout/Butte	More Difficult	10 miles	Full or Multiday	118
Sheep Spring Point	Easier	3 miles[2]	Half-day	116
Woods Canyon Lake	Easier	4 miles[2]	Half-day	118

REGION 4: SOUTHERN ARIZONA

Chiricahua	Easier to More Difficult	Variable	Half to Multiday	125
Mount Graham	Easier to More Difficult	Variable	Half to Multiday	128
Mount Lemmon	Easier to More Difficult	Variable	Short to Half-day	121

†Mileage is round trip unless otherwise indicated.
*Often skiable in low snow years.
[1]Mileage from Lockett Meadow.
[2]Mileage one way.
[3]Mileage from Sheep Crossing.

Book design by Richard Firmage
Cover design by David Jenney
Maps by Lisa Dunning and Greg Boydston
Typography by Flag Stamp and Engraving
Printing by Northland Printing Company